IRISH SEA SHIPPING

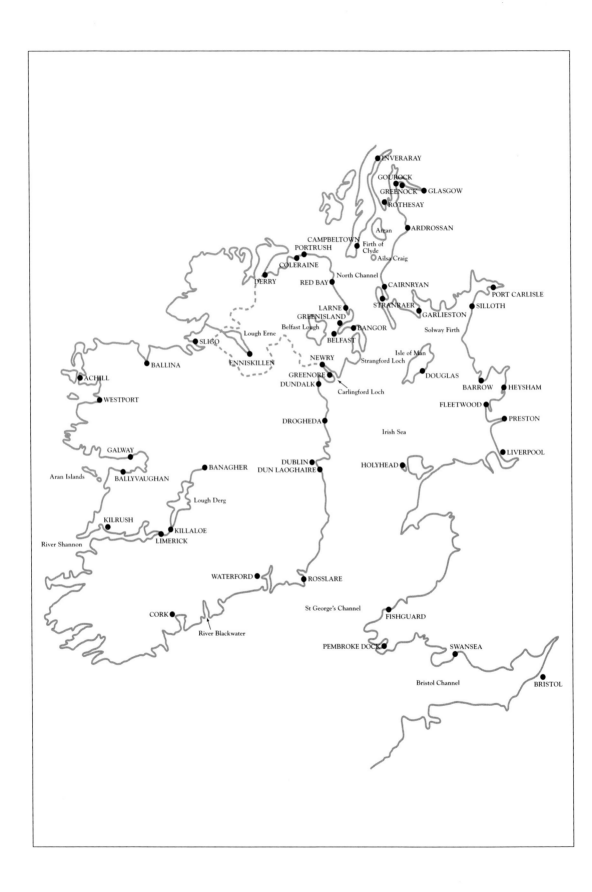

IRISH SEA SHIPPING

'Tha mile long air Cuan Eirinn'
'A thousand ships are on the Irish Sea'

Brian Patton

· MARITIME HERITAGE ·
from
○ The CUMHA Collection ○

First published in 2007

British Library Cataloguing in Publication Data

A catalogue record for this book is available from the British Library.

ISBN 978 1 85794 271 2

Silver Link Publishing Ltd
The Trundle
Ringstead Road
Great Addington
Kettering
Northants NN14 4BW

Tel/Fax: 01536 330588
email: sales@nostalgiacollection.com
Website: www.nostalgiacollection.com

Printed and bound in the Czech Republic

◦ *The CUMHA Collection* ◦

is an imprint of Silver Link Publishing Ltd

This is Donegall Quay, Belfast, in 1923/4, the heyday of cross-channel services. Nearest the camera is *Woodcock*, built for the Glasgow service in 1906 but often employed from Ardrossan, due to her comparative lack of speed. She became *Lairdswood* in 1929 but was sold in the following year to the Aberdeen SN Company, which renamed her *Lochnagar*. Beyond her lies a Fleetwood steamer, either *Duke of Cumberland* or *Duke of Argyll*, ahead of which is one of the Heysham steamers. Then there is another Burns & Laird ship and, furthest from the camera, is the Liverpool boat, *Graphic*, *Heroic* or *Patriotic*. The Burns-Laird ships wear the old Laird Line colours of white, red and black funnel, while the funnels of two LMS vessels have the yellow, red and black livery that was carried immediately after the grouping of 1923. On the right is the pier from which the Bangor boat sailed; by this date the service was being maintained by the former Blackpool paddle steamer *Greyhound*, an almost-sister of the former *Slieve Bearnagh*. *McLean Museum & Art Gallery, Inverclyde Council*

CONTENTS

PREFACE

As will be seen from the references at the end of this book, there is already a considerable literature on ships of the Irish Sea and Irish coastal and inland waters, and it may be thought that a further book on this theme is superfluous. I have therefore tried in this account to look at some lesser-known topics of this part of maritime history, in particular the part played by the London & North Western Railway. I have also tried to set the various aspects in their political and social context, within the general framework of the sometimes troubled but always close and always interesting history of the relationship between the two islands that these ships linked.

Generally speaking, the period covered is 1880 to 1980, with some exceptions at either end. It is in no sense a technical history, nor does it seek to be a complete account of the shipping lines concerned, but I hope it will bring as much pleasure to the reader as these ships have brought to myself and to countless others over the years, from childhood trips on *Lairds Isle* to recent cruising on *Lady of Mann*. Although Isle of Man steamers do appear in the book, I have not covered them in any great detail, as they have been well documented in the last year in connexion with the IOMSP Company's 175th anniversary. I hope those who particularly love Manx ships will understand! It will be appreciated that some early photographs are not of a high standard, but have been included for their interest.

It should be noted that, until 1916, Irish time was 25 minutes behind Greenwich Mean Time, and unless otherwise stated all times are given in local time. Thus a ship shown as arriving in Belfast at 2.10pm was actually arriving at 2.35pm GMT. Until 1920 Dun Laoghaire was Kingstown, and Cobh was Queenstown; the names used for these towns are those that applied during the period concerned.

Short bibliographies are given for each chapter at the end of the book, together with a general list applicable to the whole book.

I have been greatly helped by the people whose names appear below, and would like to extend to all of them my warmest thanks:

Mrs Val Boa, McLean Museum, Greenock; Don Byrne and John MacGovern, Drogheda; Sarah Canham and Rogan Dixon, National Railway Museum, York; Andrew Chong and Colin Starkey, National Maritime Museum; Miles R. Cowsill, Ferry Publications, Ramsey; Capt F. Devaney, Dalkey; T. J. Edgington, York; Simon Fountain and Norman Lee, London & North Western Railway Society; Iain D. O. Frew, Electric Railway Society; George Gardner, Glasgow University Archives; Mrs A. Gleave, National Museums Liverpool, Merseyside Maritime Museum; Dr A. C. Harper, Glasgow; Tom Hart, Beith; Fran Hegarty, Sligo County Libraries; Claudia Jew, Mariners' Museum, Newport News, Virginia; Alan McCartney, Ulster Folk & Transport Museum; Dougie Mathieson, National Library of Scotland; Alan W. H. Pearsall, Greenwich; Capt C. Puxley, Silloth; Sarah Riddle, Lancaster City Museums; Gareth Rowlands and Alf Pritchard, Holyhead; Gregg Ryan, Heritage Officer, Iarnrod Eireann, Dublin; Tony Smith, Deal, World Ship Society; Sara Smythe and Aran O'Reilly, National Library of Ireland; Michael Walker, Hest Bank; Carol Wilson and Erin Jones, Ucheldre Centre, Holyhead; the staff of the Central Library, Waterford City Libraries; the staff of the Glasgow Room, the Mitchell Library, Glasgow; and the staffs of the Ucheldre Centre, Holyhead, and the Maritime Museum, Holyhead.

Brian Patton
Foulden, Berwickshire

1  MITCHELL'S CIGARETTES.   S.S. "PUMA."

2 MITCHELL'S CIGARETTES.   S.S. "TIGER."

3 MITCHELL'S CIGARETTES.   S.S. "PATRIOTIC."

4 MITCHELL'S CIGARETTES.   S.S. "LADY LIMERICK."

5 MITCHELL'S CIGARETTES.   R.M.S. "WOODCOCK."

6 MITCHELL'S CIGARETTES.   S.S. "ST. ANDREW."

7 MITCHELL'S CIGARETTES.   S.S. "KILLARNEY."

8 MITCHELL'S CIGARETTES.   R.M.S. "DUKE OF CUMBERLAND."

9 MITCHELL'S CIGARETTES.   S.S. "GOODWIN."

10 MITCHELL'S CIGARETTES.   S.S. "BRORA."

In 1925 the Glasgow tobacco firm of Stephen Mitchell published a series of 70 cigarette cards of river and coastal steamers. Although small, many are well drawn and the colours of the various shipping companies are accurately depicted.

1   *Puma* of Burns & Laird Lines, at that date on the Dublin service. She wears the red, white and black funnel, the former Laird Line colours, at that time used by the merged fleet.

1. SHIPS OF THE SHORT SEA ROUTE, STRANRAER-LARNE, 1889-1939

Princess Victoria (1889) and Princess May (1892)

In 1889 the service between Stranraer and Larne was being maintained by two fairly small ships, *Princess Louise* of 1872 and *Princess Beatrice* of 1878. Neither was now in her prime, and when the former was repaired at Holyhead in the winter of 1885/6, at a cost of £170, Admiral Dent of the LNWR sadly reported that nothing could be done to fit her for an improved service. In 1889 a committee was formed to obtain designs for a new steamer for the service, and it was instructed to confer with Admiral Dent at Holyhead over these. On 30 May tenders were received from nine yards, and, although not quite the cheapest, the order went to Denny Bros of Dumbarton, thus starting an association that would last for more than 70 years. Prices ranged between £45,000 (J. Reid & Co) and £68,000 (J. & G. Thomson). Several firms had offered cheaper tenders for a twin-screw ship, but the committee decided that one that would cope with Loch Ryan's shallows would not

be a good sea boat, and it was decided to keep to paddle propulsion. No doubt Denny's experience with the building of the Belgian *Princesse Henriette* in the previous year was put to good use when making the tender for this ship. The payment of £46,500 was to be made in four instalments, and in the event the final price was more than £47,000.

The new ship, which was less glamorous than the Oostende vessel, was, according to her first master, Captain Campbell, essentially a cattle boat with some passenger accommodation. Nonetheless the builders took the same pains with her as they had done with the Belgian ship, and very extensive tests were undertaken in their tank to obtain the best hull form, Captain Campbell being closely involved with these.

The after deckhouse on the promenade deck contained a smoke room, with seats of perforated wood, and four 1st Class cabins were in the midships deckhouse. Forward of this was a finely upholstered general saloon. On the main deck aft were a ladies' cabin for nine, a gentlemen's cabin for four and (presumably) a dining saloon.

2 *Tiger* wearing the Coast Lines funnel and shown on one of her Scottish cruises.

3 *Patriotic* with the red and black funnel of the Belfast SS Company.

4 *Lady Limerick* shows the green and black colour scheme of the British & Irish SP Company.

5 Although by this date a member of the merged Burns & Laird fleet, *Woodcock* is shown in the rather gloomy all-over black of the Burns ships.

6 The very tall red and black funnels denote that *St Andrew* sails for the Great Western Railway.

7 *Killarney* (ex-*Magic*) is shown as a member of the City of Cork SP Company's fleet, with its white and black funnels.

8 After experimenting with the L&YR's yellow, red and black funnels, the LMS settled for the former LNWR yellow with black, as shown on the Fleetwood turbine steamer *Duke of Cumberland*.

9 *Goodwin* of the Clyde Shipping Company was then employed on the Glasgow-Belfast-London route. The black hull and funnel are relieved by white upperworks. This vessel was built in 1917 and immediately requisitioned as a decoy (or Q) ship, not entering her owner's service until 1919.

10 Often seen on the Irish Sea were the black and white funnels of the ships of William Sloan & Co of Glasgow. Although the firm originally had connections with Belfast, by this date its ships served Glasgow and Bristol only. Seen here is *Brora*, built in 1924 and scrapped in 1959.

Above   Princess Victoria. National Maritime Museum

Left Princess May leaving Stranraer. Author's collection

Steerage passengers were accommodated forward on the main deck, and their quarters were separated from those for 700 cattle and several horses by a canvas screen. On trial on 22 April she attained a satisfactory 19.75 knots against a head wind.

Named *Princess Victoria*, this new ship brought a considerable improvement to the Stranraer-Larne service, not only in her own facilities and increased reliability, but also in the provision of a new 'daylight' service, based on Larne. This allowed a fairly quick journey between Glasgow and Belfast and vice versa; passengers could leave Belfast at 9.00am and be in Glasgow at 4.00pm. In the reverse direction, a departure at the civilised hour of 9.50am allowed passengers to be in Belfast at 4.00pm. New carriages were built for the trains connecting with these sailings, and it spelled competition for Messrs Burns's daylight service, which was slightly faster but had a longer sea passage.

In 1892 *Princess Victoria* met up with *Adder*

when returning from overhaul in Belfast and raced her as far as Ailsa Craig. There was no definite winner, but no doubt the crews and the passengers on *Adder* enjoyed the sport. Whatever their respective merits, the travelling public liked the new service, which carried 10,200 passengers during its first summer and became a regular feature of the timetable thereafter.

The only weak point of the new ship lay in her paddle wheels, which constantly gave trouble and almost led to disaster in September 1892. When crossing from Larne she met the full force of a gale, and when she had almost entered Loch Ryan a float on the port wheel became loose. As it was impossible to repair this in such weather, the captain dropped anchor and the ship stopped in Port Mullen Bay, near Corsewall Point. In due course she was rescued by her sister, *Princess May*, but the tired and probably seasick passengers did not reach Stranraer until 9.30pm instead of 12.20pm.

Later that year Denny replaced the steel floats

by wheels of wrought iron and the sponsons were strengthened. This seems to have cured that particular problem, but there were others that persisted throughout the life of the steamer. No doubt Denny applied the lessons learned when building both her sister ship and also later Belgian paddle steamers.

Princess Victoria's sister ship was *Princess May* of 1892, a virtual repeat and at the same price, but with stronger paddle wheels and a small shelter deck around the funnels. In service she proved to be more reliable, and her only major accident came when she was not actually in service. During a gale on 22 December 1894 she was driven so far up on to the beach at Stranraer that it took three weeks to free her, with the aid of tugs. The whole episode cost the joint committee £2,700; it then transpired that their underwriter had absconded across the English Channel and the committee had to foot the bill themselves.

In 1897 sleeping berths were fitted to both ships, to allow passengers to stay on board overnight at Stranraer. Four years later both were thoroughly examined by Captain Binney from

Princess Maud (1904) in LMS colours at Stranraer. *Author's collection*

Holyhead and his verdict was that they had only about three years of front-line work left. He suggested reboilering, but the committee shied away from the expense involved and instead decided in 1903 to seek tenders to replace *Princess Beatrice*, now totally outclassed and attracting unwelcome interest from the Board of Trade on account of the state of her boilers. *Princess Victoria* was scrapped in 1910, but *Princess May* remained in service until 1912, then had two more years as reserve ship before being sold to the Admiralty in October 1914. Her career finally came to an end in 1922.

Princess Maud (1904)

In June 1903 a turbine steamer was ordered from Denny at a price of £66,000, the first with this type of propulsion to be used on any Irish Sea service. The new ship was named *Princess Maud* and the new machinery, which worked well in service, brought about a considerable change in the layout of her accommodation. The 1st Class was now amidships and steerage was moved to the stern, where passengers could feel the full effects of the vibration, which was one of the very few problems of the ship. However, their facilities were very

Princess Maud (1904) in LMS colours approaching Stranraer on the mail run. On summer evenings this sailing often provided the opportunity to enjoy a marvellous sunset over the Irish coast or in Loch Ryan. *Author's collection*

much better, with a ladies' lounge on the poop deck, a combined lounge and tearoom on the main deck below, and yet another lounge on the lower deck. Steerage passengers were still rather near the cattle, most of which were in pens on those decks aft, but at least they were now separated from the animals by a bulkhead rather than just a canvas curtain. For those in 1st Class there was a ladies' cabin, a bar, some private staterooms and a dormitory on the promenade deck, and a dining saloon and more cabins on the main deck.

In service *Princess Maud* ran well but was a rather unlucky ship. On 30 November 1906 she was hit by an enormous wave when crossing from Larne, which flooded her after deck and injured three passengers. Worse was to come. On 6 August 1909, when proceeding down Loch Ryan in a thick sea mist, she cut into and sank the small passenger/cargo steamer *Pirate*. The crew, the four passengers and a cat were all rescued, mostly by the *Maud* herself, but one lady, who was in poor health, later died. An out-of-court settlement cost the joint committee £2,600. Then on 9 June 1910 she rammed the pier at Larne so hard that she tore a large hole in her port bow; after this incident all steamers reversed into Larne. However, her luck changed during the war and, despite the submarine presence in the Irish Sea, she led a charmed life. When, on one occasion, she was given an escort of two aged destroyers, she

completely outran them! Her luck held almost to the end of her career, but ran out just before she did. In fog on 9 June 1931 she ran hard on to Island Magee just outside Larne. All the passengers were taken off in the lifeboats and landed on the island, then caught the local ferry to Larne. The ship pulled herself off the next morning, but her career was over and she was sold to the shipbreakers for £2,500.

Princess Victoria (1912)

Princess May was by 1911 clearly reaching the end of her useful life, and to replace her another turbine was ordered from Denny. She was almost a sister ship to *Princess Maud*, one of the main differences being that provision for stowage of motor cars was incorporated into her design. As *Princess Victoria* she took up service in April 1912, and despite arduous war service as a troopship out of Dover she seemed to be a very lucky ship. Twice she was attacked by U-boats and one torpedo passed within inches of her hull: 'No hero met death on her decks, but many met it gloriously just over her gangways,' according to later LMS publicity. The breakers claimed her in 1934.

Princess Margaret (1931)

The entry into service of this much-improved ship, again from Denny, was marked by a lunch in the Laharna Hotel, Larne, on 31 March 1931, after which she took the invited guests across to Stranraer and proved to be remarkably steady in quite a choppy sea. An attractive feature was an

Above *Princess Victoria* (1912) in LMS colours passing Finnart on Loch Ryan. *Author's collection*

Right There could be no doubt that *Princess Margaret* was a coal-burner as she backed out of Stranraer in September 1936! *J. Sutherland, author's collection*

Right Apart from serving with distinction as a Landing Ship (Infantry) from March to October 1944, *Princess Margaret*'s war service was the vital role of keeping her own route open. She carried thousands of military personnel and civilians during this period, being assisted by a variety of other cross-channel ships, but it was normally she who took the mail run. She had an austerity refit in the winter of 1944 and resumed service at Stranraer on Christmas Day, to continue virtually single-handed until her sister came back in September 1945 to relieve her. This view shows her in wartime grey at Belfast. *National Maritime Museum*

observation lounge, forward on the boat deck, furnished with glass-topped wicker tables and Lloyd Loom chairs. The smoke room was aft on this deck and a lounge occupied the promenade deck forward. The dining saloon was aft on this deck, with a view over the hold; it was furnished in a restrained Art Deco style, with tables for four or six on which were attractive shaded lamps. Cabin accommodation in 1st Class was for 107, a great improvement over the 28 in older ships. Cattle, of course, were not neglected, and stalls could be erected for 236 animals, together with eight permanent horse stalls. The final price was £179,346 plus £390 for the wireless equipment. *Princess Margaret* had a long and successful career, almost all being spent on the route for which she was built, until sold to Hong Kong owners in 1962. There, as *Macau*, she served equally well until wrecked in a typhoon in August 1971.

Princess Maud (1934)

While the arrival of *Princess Margaret* at Stranraer certainly attracted passengers to the service, it also highlighted the drawbacks of *Princess Victoria*, which now seemed to be totally out of date, and it was therefore decided to order another new ship to provide a uniform standard of service. Again the order went to Denny, and in 1934 the second *Princess Maud* took her place on the service. Prices having fallen, she was rather cheaper than her sister, at £160,000.

In most respects she followed the design of the latter. There was an observation lounge on the upper deck, although it lacked the little tables – perhaps these had been liable to topple over in a rough sea. Aft of the lounge were eight two-berth and eight single-berth cabins and two two-berth special cabins, which shared a bathroom and toilet. The smoke room was aft on this deck and was furnished with a fireplace and about 40 seats in the form of modern tub armchairs. On the promenade deck forward was the 1st Class lounge complete with large, clumsy armchairs upholstered in an Art Deco pattern, and, on the port side, a ladies' lounge with 11 seats. Aft of the entrance with the purser's bureau were 12 more two-berth cabins and 11 single-berth cabins, with two bathrooms and separate ladies' and gentlemen's lavatories. A novel feature that passengers

probably appreciated was that all two-berth cabins in 1st Class had the berths side by side, instead of one above the other. The dining saloon, with 76 places, had a view over the hold, aft of which the deckhouse accommodated baggage and mail rooms and, for those travelling 3rd Class, a ladies' room with ten berths and a smoke room and bar.

Amidships on the main deck were 49 more 1st Class cabins, stalls for 30 cattle and 12 horses, and cabins for the captain and officers. Aft, a general room could take about 100 passengers in 3rd Class. The lower deck midships section had 12 more 1st Class cabins and crew accommodation. Forward were stalls for 81 cattle and aft were the only 3rd Class cabins, six four-berth and three two-berth. There were also two open cabins for gentlemen, each with ten berths. Throughout the ship the woodwork and furnishings were to a particularly high standard and, for the service for which she was designed, she was a comfortable vessel.

However, her greatest claim to fame was that she was the first channel steamer to be fitted with a Ginnel automatic sprinkler system. This worked from a tank with a capacity of 1,000 gallons. During what surely was a most unusual press trip, a two-berth 3rd Class cabin on the main deck was used to give a demonstration of the system, the wash basin first being removed. Each berth was covered with pitch pine shavings and, to ensure a good blaze, these were then liberally sprinkled with naphtha and a match applied to the lower berth. Flames shot out to a distance of about 4 feet from the partially closed door, but these were extinguished in 15-20 seconds. Very little remained of the curtains, but the bulkhead was only damaged to the extent of the top layer of paint, and there was no structural damage.

With *Princess Margaret*, *Princess Maud* brought about a considerable upsurge in traffic on the Stranraer-Larne service, passenger numbers climbing from a total of 134,038 in 1929 to 219,341 in 1938. In the winter of 1937-38 additional seating was fitted and her dining accommodation improved, and in the following winter she was converted by her builders to oil-firing. But it was to be her misfortune to serve most of her career on a different service, for which she had insufficient accommodation, particularly for those in 3rd Class. After a distinguished war record, including several trips to Dunkirk and participation in the D-Day landings, she had a brief spell back at Stranraer until transferred to Holyhead in February 1947, the LMS authorities seeing in her a partial solution to the problems posed by the ageing, coal-burning mail boats. She was based there for the rest of her career, though occasionally relieving on other services such as Fishguard-Waterford and Heysham-Belfast, and made her last sailing on 4 September 1965.

Despite some re-arrangement of her accommodation to give a total of 202 berths, this was inadequate for the numbers travelling at peak periods and she became known in Dublin as the '— Princess Maud'. In 3rd Class there were only 80 berths in cabins and open saloons and, indeed, only about 150 other passengers in that class could expect to find a seat under cover. The other 300-plus had to make do with a seat on the stairs or simply lie down on the deck – such experiences did not encourage customer loyalty! Even the 1954 Irish Services joint timetable was reticent about her; after enthusing about the 'fine post-war motor vessels' that 'give an impression of an ocean liner', it mentioned only that she had sleeping accommodation for 202 passengers.

She was sold to Greek owners in 1965 and, as Venus, sailed for some years on services to Cyprus and Israel. Later she became an accommodation ship in Copenhagen as Nybo and was finally scrapped in 1974.

Princess Maud (1934) alongside Carlisle Pier, Dun Laoghaire, on 30 July 1964. *Author*

2. THE COMING OF
THE CAR FERRY

It is not recorded when the first motor car was shipped from Britain to Ireland, but it must have been at quite an early date. By 1912 facilities for taking cars and motorcycles via Stranraer-Larne were being advertised, suggesting that the traffic was already significant. In August of that year alone, 120 cars crossed on this service. Vehicles were of course craned aboard and had to be alongside the ship 1 hour before sailing time. The charges were based on weight, beginning with cars up to 10cwt, which cost £1 5s 0d per single journey, a figure that represented about half of a reasonable weekly wage. No separate annual figures were given for the number actually conveyed but, apart from the war years, this continued to increase and in 1927 600 cars were conveyed in July and August alone. Ten years later 4,000 cars were carried, and the loading and unloading of these was affecting timekeeping.

Of course other cross-channel lines were also experiencing similar problems. The British & Irish Steam Packet Company, at that time trading as Irish Free State Lines, was decidedly more expensive, as the charge for a 10cwt car from Liverpool to Dublin was £3, although a return fare of £4 10s 0d was offered when two passengers accompanied the car. B&I publicity showed a rather elderly upright saloon car being hoisted aboard, while LMS publicity for other routes suggested that cars were carefully covered by a tarpaulin while being shipped.

It was time to have a ship dedicated to car traffic, using roll-on/roll-off facilities, but one that could also function as a normal passenger ferry as necessary, and in January 1938 the LMS Board decided to commission one. The contract went to Denny, and in April 1939 the third *Princess Victoria* was launched. As there was no precedent in Western Europe for such a vessel built new, Denny had to start from scratch. The yard produced a design in which almost the entire main deck was given over to vehicles, all the passenger

The stern of *Princess Victoria* (1939) seen while she was in dry dock in Glasgow in June 1939. *National Maritime Museum*

Princess Victoria on trials on the Clyde on 26 June 1939.
Author's collection

accommodation being on the promenade and upper decks. Two classes were catered for, each having a lounge bar and dining saloon, and there were only six cabins, on the boat deck. Passenger numbers were 875 in 1st Class and 542 in 3rd. The main deck could take 80 cars, and there were also sheep pens forward of the engine room casing, with cattle pens on the lower deck. Two turntables on the main deck allowed cars to be turned ready for disembarkation, and there was also emergency crane access via hatches. Diesel engines (Sulzer) were an innovation for a large railway ship.

Of course, commissioning the ship was only part of the equation. Ramps had to be provided at both ports, this being more complicated at Larne where dual-gauge railway tracks crossed the ramp at right angles, but the relatively low tidal range of 9 feet meant that the length of the ramps could be confined to 60 feet at Stranraer and 70 feet at Larne. Parking and marshalling areas were also laid out, and the entire operation cost the LMS almost £200,000, to which had to be added the £190,860 5s 5d cost of the ship, which was in fact £4,000 over the contract price. All went according to plan, however, and on 7 July *Princess Victoria* entered service on the Larne-based roster, leaving that port at 10.08am Monday-Thursday and at 8.05am and 2.50pm on Friday and Saturday. She also undertook one cruise from Stranraer, around Ailsa Craig, on Wednesday 19 July.

All seemed to be set for a successful career, but war intervened and on 31 August the ship made her final crossings, being requisitioned by the Admiralty immediately and fitted out for minelaying. She was successful in this also, often working in stormy conditions, and laid a total of 2,756 mines. However, on 18 May 1940, when returning to her base in the Humber, she struck a German mine and sank with the loss of 34 of her crew. Although in very shallow water and on an upright keel, she was beyond salvage.

Nevertheless, in her short life she had amply demonstrated the potential of a car ferry service, and as early as December 1944 the LMS decided to replace her, giving the order again to Denny. The new *Princess Victoria* was ready in March 1947, and on the 18th she took up service on the normal mail run, services having been disrupted due to blizzard conditions. The car ferry service began in May and during the remainder of the summer almost 3,000 cars were carried.

Little can be added here to what has already been written about this ship. However, it may be pointed out that, having been given some passenger accommodation – a lounge and cabins – forward on the main deck, she was the first dual-purpose car ferry in British waters, contemporary car ferries on the English Channel being restricted to motor cars and accompanying passengers only. She had berths for 54 in 1st Class. These features reduced her car capacity to 70 but did allow her to take the mail service when necessary. In 1949 her car deck was strengthened to allow her to carry milk tankers, and thus she also became a commercial vehicle carrier.

It was this feature of the passenger accommodation on the main deck that allowed her to stay afloat for so long after her stern door had been breached on 31 January 1953, as it was almost 2 hours before the water could extend for the entire length of the hull and cause a fatal list. While many lessons were learned from the disaster, the value of such a barrier on a vessel's car

The 1st Class lounge of *Princess Victoria* of 1947. It was always expected that passengers in 1st Class would wish to write letters, and the writing desk, which would later be provided with notepaper and envelopes, can just be seen on the left. *Glasgow University Archives*

deck was not one of them. But the tragedy of her end should not obscure the fact that *Princess Victoria* was a success story until that fatal day.

Following the disaster, a kind of paralysis seems to have gripped the upper echelons of the British Transport Commission regarding the service, although local management was strengthened. It was not until January 1957 that it was announced that a new ship was to be built, but in 1958 this was countermanded and it was not until September 1959 that an order was actually placed with Denny's yard for a replacement. The stop-gap solution was to bring the train ferry ship *Hampton Ferry* round from Dover each summer to work the Larne-based roster. Cars travelled on her train deck, with planks laid over the rails, as her own garage on the upper deck could not be reached from the shore installations at either port. Despite her limitations in the matter of accommodation

and speed – she required 2¾ hours for the passage – the number of cars carried by her continually increased, from 2,500 in 1953 to 6,600 in 1956.

When the new ship finally arrived, it was at once obvious that all the lobbying carried out by local people, politicians and staff had not been in vain – *Caledonian Princess* was beyond doubt the finest ship ever to grace the crossing. She had space for 100 cars and 70 cattle, 400 1st and 1,000 2nd Class passengers, with cabin accommodation for 82 in 1st and 94 in 2nd Class. She was fitted with twin rudders, the latest type of stabilisers and a bow thrust unit. Her second master, Captain Leslie Unsworth, took great delight in showing her off to visitors, sometimes to the surprise of the engine room staff, who wondered why the stabilisers were being activated in a perfectly calm Loch Ryan!

But perhaps it was in the furnishings of the ship that the greatest advance was made. In matters of passenger numbers and vehicles carried, there was no doubt about the appeal of the new ship; in 1963 46,000 vehicles and 300,000 passengers used the route, giving a profit of £370,000 and removing the threat that the new ship would be transferred to

Above and right Bow and stern views of *Hampton Ferry* alongside at Stranraer in August 1960. *Tom Hart*

Below Caledonian Princess leaving Larne on 2 August 1964. *Author*

ADDITIONAL
drive on - drive off
SERVICES
for motor cars

between

GREAT BRITAIN

and

NORTHERN IRELAND

via Stranraer and Larne

by Motor Vessel
"SLIEVE DONARD"

DAILY—MONDAYS TO SATURDAYS
6th JULY to 24th AUGUST, 1964

NOTE.—The Sailings shown in this folder are in addition
to the advertised "Caledonian Princess" Car Ferry Service
which operates twice daily in each direction between
Stranraer and Larne throughout the year.

Above left The stern of *Caledonian Princess*, seen at Larne.
The door that covered the stern at sea is seen in its open
position. *Author*

Above A handbill advertising the additional service. *Author's
collection*

Left Passengers and bystanders watch with interest as a van
is driven on board *Slieve Donard* at Larne in 1964.
Nowadays health and safety regulations would not allow
scenes of this kind. *Author*

another route if she did not make a profit. By 1964, indeed, she was the victim of her own success and for that summer the cargo ship *Slieve Donard* had to be chartered from British Railways. As she could not carry passengers, they travelled in *Caledonian Princess* and, after waiting for some time, were reunited with their cars on the other side. It was not an ideal arrangement, nor was that of the charter of a larger German ship, *Lohengrin*, in 1965.

In 1966 it was finally accepted that a car/passenger ship was required, and *Stena Nordica*, which had been sailing on a Tilbury-Calais service, was chartered from Stena Line. She lacked stabilisers and, being rather broad in the beam, had a propensity to roll, but she had bright Scandinavian décor internally and introduced to the route the benefit of a bow door. More and more commercial vehicles were being carried, and these were now of larger dimensions. Manoeuvring these on and off the *Princess* called for skill on the part of all concerned and sometimes held up the ship.

This feature was therefore included in the next ship to be built for the route. *Antrim Princess* was built on the Tyne by Hawthorn, Leslie and

Stena Nordica **at Larne on 3 September 1969.** *T. J. Edgington*

entered service in December 1967. She also copied the Stena ship in having diesel propulsion and a height of more than 14 feet on the vehicle deck. Two portable mezzanine decks were also fitted. Although pleasant, the design of her accommodation lacked the flair shown in that of *Caledonian Princess*. With the arrival of the new vessel, the latter was removed from Stranraer and began a peripatetic career around British ports, finally ending up at Dover, from where, in September 1981, she was to be the last steamship to cross the English Channel in regular service.

British Railways seemed to be even more hesitant as far as its other services were concerned. The Heysham steamers were replaced by classic passenger ships in 1956/7, but these were really ships of the 1940s and made no allowance for the growth in the use of the private car, let alone commercial vehicles. When BR finally realised that it could not go on running passenger-only ships for ever, the need to cater for the car was, in most cases, met by somewhat piecemeal conversions of existing ships, which then did not cater properly for either class of traffic. The Heysham 'Dukes' were successively converted, and at Fishguard *Saint David* became a side-loading car ferry in 1965.

Above Cars being driven on to *Antrim Princess* through the bow door at Stranraer on 6 September 1969. The Western SMT coach, AAG 100B, is a Leyland Leopard with an Alexander dual-purpose body, delivered in 1964. *T. J. Edgington*

Left *Antrim Princess* sailing serenely up Loch Ryan in May 1981. *Author*

Below *Duke of Lancaster*, as converted to a car ferry, at Carlisle Pier, Dun Laoghaire, on 30 August 1979. *Author*

Traffic continued to grow at Fishguard, and in 1971 the magnificent *Avalon*, from the Harwich-Hoek route, which had been converted to a car ferry, was transferred to the Irish Sea, serving at both Fishguard and Holyhead. She was not well maintained while on those services and attracted criticism in the motoring press for her untidy and dirty internal condition. She went for scrap at the early age of 17 in 1980. She is seen here at Fishguard. *Miles R. Cowsill*

Only the Holyhead-Dun Laoghaire service was given the benefit of a new, purpose-built ship when *Holyhead Ferry I* appeared in 1966. While such unimaginative names are common on ferries now, this attracted much adverse comment at the time, and in due course the ship became *Earl Leofric*. In the event, she was not ready for the start of the service on 9 July 1965 and the quick transfer of *Normannia* from Dover instituted the practice of regularly switching car ferries between the English Channel and the Irish Sea. Even on this service the initial shore facilities seemed to be of a stop-gap nature, with a somewhat primitive ramp being constructed at St Michael's Wharf, Dun Laoghaire. At Holyhead a ramp was constructed on the Admiralty Pier, near the former mailboat berth. It was not until the end of the 1970s that BR at last began to build new ships that would be suitable for the Irish Sea traffic.

The Coast Lines group seemed to be equally at a loss as to how to deal with the motor vehicle, other than to offer shipment on conventional passenger ships. This was relatively expensive – the single rate for a small car (up to 10cwt) on the Glasgow-Belfast route in 1954 was £8. Apart from the cost, the loading and unloading times were inconvenient. For a departure at 9.00pm, cars had to be alongside the vessel before 6.30pm, except on summer Fridays when the time was 3.30pm! No times were shown for unloading cars at the destination. The first tentative step was taken in 1965 when, between trips on the Ardrossan-Belfast route, *Scottish Coast* was fitted by workmen from her builders, A. Stephen & Co, with a lift on the fore deck and altered internally to carry about 25 cars. It was a very makeshift conversion and was reversed after *Lion* entered service.

Publicity material for *Holyhead Ferry I*. *Author's collection*

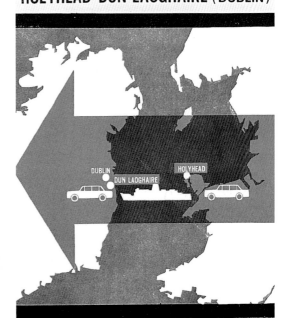

new
IRISH FERRY
for cars
HOLYHEAD-DUN LAOGHAIRE (DUBLIN)

DUBLIN
DUN LAOGHAIRE
HOLYHEAD

Starting 9 July 1965
DRIVE-ON DRIVE-OFF TO IRELAND
British Railways
LONDON MIDLAND REGION

Top Holyhead Ferry *I* at Heysham in August 1970. *T. J. Edgington*

Above Dover, her near sister, was one of the first ships from the English Channel to come to the Irish Sea, in 1969, and is seen here arriving at Heysham from Dun Laoghaire on 30 July 1970. On the left is *Saint David*, which had been brought up to operate a Heysham-Dun Laoghaire service. *T. J. Edgington*

Left The freight ferry *Dalriada* at St Michael's Wharf, Dun Laoghaire, in August 1979. *Author*

At Liverpool the Belfast SS Company grasped the nettle in 1965 and ordered two dual-purpose ships, one each from Harland & Wolff and Cammell Laird, at a cost of almost £2 million each. They were in effect financed by the sale of the British & Irish Steam Packet Company to the government of Ireland. They were extremely comfortable ships, with two-class accommodation, and continued to provide a civilised travelling environment long after other companies had given up on the concept. Sadly they had little space for commercial vehicles. Named *Ulster Queen* and *Ulster Prince*, they entered service on 6 June and 19 April 1967 respectively. The service ended amid bitter industrial wrangling in November 1981 and both ships were sold to Cypriot owners.

Lion, the first and, as events turned out, the only Burns & Laird car ferry, was an excellent ship, with plenty of seating accommodation, a restaurant and separate cafeteria, and wide deck space. The rather formal publicity of former years was now cast aside in favour of something emphasising the carefree, holiday atmosphere, with slogans such as 'Clearway to adventure', 'Children have lots of fun' or 'Your holiday begins

Scottish Coast at Anderston Quay in Glasgow; ahead are a cargo vessel and one of the 'Royal' sisters, and beyond again is the Finnieston vehicle ferry. Nearer the camera the Clyde Street passenger ferry is doing good business, with two boats in service. *Author's collection*

the moment you drive aboard!' A through express coach service to Dublin was offered and a publicity film, 'In the Lion's Wake', was widely circulated. The daylight service, for the first time in its history, was now year-round, and the ship also gave night freight-only sailings to Larne. Sadly all this effort was to come to naught, not through any defect in the ship herself but because of the increasing violence in the north of Ireland. Freight held up reasonably well, but passenger numbers evaporated and in February 1976 the service was withdrawn, *Lion* going off to start a new service for P&O in the English Channel. Effectively this was not only the end of the passenger daylight service, but was also the end of Burns & Laird Lines and a tradition going back to 1824. It was a sad ending and should not have happened this way.

A most interesting venture began in 1971 when Western Ferries, a Scottish company that had been trying to compete with David MacBrayne on routes to Islay, began a service between Campbeltown in Argyll and Red Bay in Antrim. The ship used, *Sound of Islay*, was fairly small and provided few creature comforts for the passenger, but she was efficient and fares were low, beginning at £4 single for a car up to 11 feet in length. There were two sailings in each direction on Mondays, Fridays, Saturdays and Sundays and one on other days; these left Campbeltown at 6.00am and 2.00pm, and 10.00am respectively. At first the service did well, but the troubles were then

Above **Ulster Queen** in P&O livery at an otherwise deserted Donegall Quay in March 1979. *Author*

Left A berth ticket, dated 4 November 1976, still shows the ship in Belfast SS Co colours, although the company had been taken over by P&O Ferries in 1971. Very shortly after this ticket was issued there was a complete change to the P&O corporate livery, to almost universal regret. *Author's collection*

Below **Lion.** *Author's collection*

Right Sound of Islay at Campbeltown in June 1973, with Caledonian MacBrayne's *Queen Mary II* blowing off steam behind. *Author*

increasing in the north of Ireland and it closed after the summer season of 1973.

As mentioned earlier, the British & Irish Steam Packet Company was sold to the government of Ireland in 1965 for £3.5 million and the new owners lost no time in preparing to introduce car ferries, both on the Dublin service and also to Cork from South Wales. Unlike the operators detailed above, there was nothing half-hearted or conventional about the conversion of the Liverpool-Dublin or what became the Swansea-Cork services. Ships, marketing and publicity all displayed a totally new approach. The company acquired an almost completed ship from German builders Werft Nobiskring in Rensburg, ordered a close sister from the new Verolme yard in Cork, and ordered another from the same German yard. These vessels in due course became *Munster*, *Leinster* and *Innisfallen*. Internal design owed much to that of Scandinavian ferries and the ships were operated on a one-class basis.

Some people would consider the new layout and décor cheap and cheerful, but others found it attractive and modern. On *Munster* all cabins were located below the car deck and there were no single-berth cabins, while the other two ships had some additional cabins on the upper deck. On the promenade deck there was a cafeteria and a lounge with reclining seats forward, a children's playroom and shop and another lounge with bar aft. On the upper deck there was a restaurant and another bar forward, and a quiet lounge aft. The other two ships had the novel feature of an observation lounge on top of the bridge and an enlarged cafeteria. Hostesses in a smart modern blue uniform greeted passengers arriving on board, and

Right Publicity material for the Campbeltown-Red Bay service. *Author's collection*

DRIVE ON DRIVE OFF TO IRELAND

SUMMER '72

Western Ferries
ANTRIM / KINTYRE

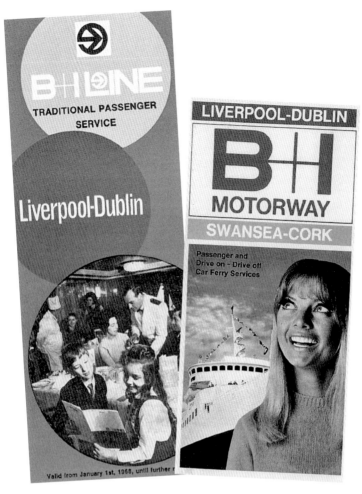

Left Publicity material for the new service, featuring *Munster*. It was all a far cry from the traditional passenger service that operated alongside her during the 1968 season. *Author's collection*

Below *Innisfallen* leaving Pembroke Dock for Cork in June 1982. She was originally *Leinster* but was renamed when transferred to the southern route in 1980. *Miles R. Cowsill*

the whole was set off by a new livery in which blue and white predominated. It was a complete break from tradition and passengers welcomed it with enthusiasm; numbers increased in a gratifying manner. An auxiliary car deck could be brought into use at peak periods and, having bow and stern doors, the new ships could turn round in port in an hour. A bow thrust unit helped when approaching or leaving port.

While all the existing operators were procrastinating, a complete newcomer to the Irish Sea was showing what could be done with vehicle ferries. The Atlantic Steam Navigation Company, under the leadership of Frank Bustard, had begun a service from Tilbury to Rotterdam using converted landing ships from the Second World War, and in May 1948 also began a service from Preston to Larne, Liverpool having rejected the company's plans to operate from that port. In 1954 ASNC became part of the British Transport Commission, but this made no difference in practice to its operation. This service prospered, although the passenger accommodation on the *Empire Cedric* was fairly basic, and in 1957 the first of two purpose-built and very handsome ferries was built by Denny.

Named *Bardic Ferry*, she provided accommodation of a high standard for two classes of passenger and this was matched by the standard of service – a white-jacketed crew member met passengers as they drove up to the ship and took their car on board. A sister ship, *Ionic Ferry*, followed in 1958. All continued to go well and the efficiency and quality of service put many existing operators to shame. However, in 1971 the Conservative government put the company up for sale and it went to European Ferries, operators of the Townsend-Thoresen fleet in the English Channel, and in 1973 the Preston-Larne service was closed and replaced by a short sea crossing to Larne from the wartime port of Cairnryan.

The service had now entered a different era, that of the modern high-capacity car ferry, operating on a high-frequency service. Various Townsend ferries were tried until in 1976 *Free Enterprise IV* was permanently assigned to it, together with ex-ASNC ships. The attractive livery of black hull with a white line, and blue funnel with a white band and black top, gave way

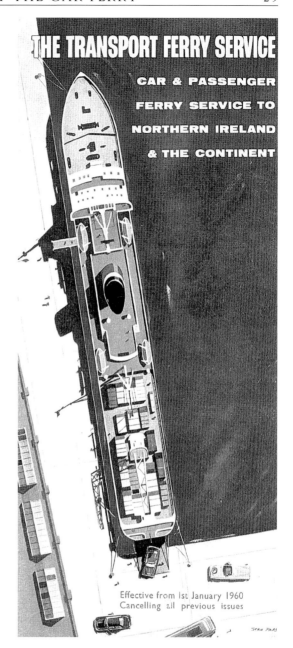

An ASNC leaflet from 1960. The single fare, in a 1st Class single-berth cabin, was £4 5s 0d, inclusive of meals, and the charge for a small car was £6 5s 0d. Sailing times varied according to the tide and the passage time was 12½ hours. *Author's collection*

to the glaring orange hull and unusual turquoise funnel of the T-T group. The era of the modern ferry had at last arrived on the Irish Sea, but there were many who regretted the passing of the more leisurely methods of operation.

"CALEDONIAN PRINCESS" LEAVING LARNE R 6251

Above Sometimes publishers of postcards got things wrong! This is definitely not the ship named on the card, which actually shows *Bardic Ferry* in her original livery. *Author's collection*

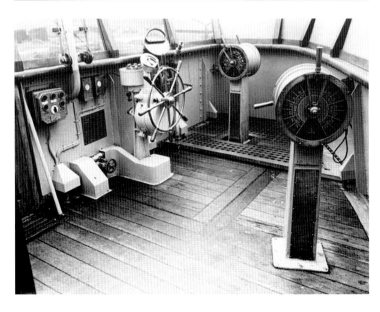

Above left and left Views of the car deck and bridge of *Bardic Ferry*. *Glasgow University Archives*

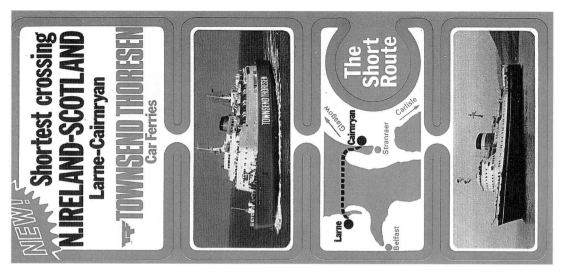

Above Ionic Ferry *in dry dock, showing her fine lines.* ASN collection, courtesy of Miles R. Cowsill

Right Publicity material for Townsend-Thoresen services in 1974. The ship featured is *Free Enterprise III*, which covered the service in 1974 only. By then there were at least three crossings in each direction per day and the charge for a single trip with a small car was £5.20, plus £1.15 for the driver. These fares were clearly an introductory offer, since they soon increased substantially, even allowing for contemporary inflation. The other ship pictured is either *Bardic* or *Ionic Ferry*. Author's collection

First Class two-berth cabin   *Dining Room*   *First Class lounge and bar*   *A four-berth cabin*

m.v. 'BARDIC FERRY' & 'IONIC FERRY'

These vessels, completed in 1957/8, provide up-to-date cabin and public room accommodation, with all amenities. Passengers are carried in either first or second class accommodation. The First Class accommodation provides two-berth and single cabins, with wardrobes, ample drawer space and hot and cold running water. The two-berth cabins are also provided with dressing tables. An excellent First Class dining room and a separate lounge and bar are available to the seventeen First Class passengers carried.

Second Class accommodation provides two- and four-berth cabins equipped with wardrobes, hot and cold water, etc.: a second class dining room and a separate lounge and bar are available to the thirty-eight passengers. Ample deck space is available to both Classes, and the amenities and service leave nothing to be desired, even to the provision of special sockets for electric razors, (220v D.C.). Full bar facilities are provided.

Passengers on the spacious sun deck

Above Publicity material for *Bardic Ferry* and *Ionic Ferry*. *Author's collection*

Below   *Free Enterprise IV* leaving Larne, with the Islandmagee ferry in the foreground, in May 1981. *Author*

The last and most luxurious member of the ASN fleet was *Europic Ferry*, built on the Tyne by Swan, Hunter in 1967. Now wearing P&O livery, she is seen in a contre-jour shot while crossing from Larne to Cairnryan on 1 December 1987. *Author*

The Isle of Man Steam Packet Company adopted the car ferry at a reasonably early date, but sadly did not then go on to develop this concept into that of a commercial vehicle ferry. With *Manx Maid* of 1962, the company first adopted the design that would allow vehicles to be driven on and off at any state of the tide, at any port, by means of a series of ramps at the stern of the ship, and went on to build three further ships to the same basic layout between then and 1976. This design saved the trouble of installing special facilities at ports and proved to be an excellent method of handling the peak traffic associated with the TT Races. However, hauliers on the island became impatient and ultimately worked with other interests to set up a new company that would provide a service taking commercial vehicles. In the end this was to lead to the downfall of the IOMSPC as an independent company after a life of more than 150 years.

The second car ferry and the last turbine steamer built for service on the Irish Sea was *Ben-My-Chree* of 1966, seen here basking in the evening sun at Douglas in July 1972. *Author*

Left Ben-My-Chree was, unusually, equipped with a steam-driven bow thrust unit, which can be seen in action as she comes alongside at Douglas in August 1982. *Author*

Below Manx Lines' first and, as it turned out, only ship was a former Aznar Line ferry, renamed *Manx Viking* (alias, to some, *The Incredible Hulk*), and seen here in the line's original colour scheme at the yard of Harland & Wolff, Belfast, in March 1979. *Author*

3. THE DAYLIGHT SERVICE

'This route will particularly appeal to those who enjoy sea travel for its own sake.' So ran a line in the Burns Laird guide of 1938. It was to a large extent true: on a good day there was much to see. After leaving Ardrossan, the coastal scenery of Ayrshire could be enjoyed for almost an hour, with fine views of Arran to starboard. The ship usually passed close to Ailsa Craig, by which point it would be time to go below for an excellent lunch. When the traveller emerged on deck once again, the coast of Antrim would be in view and there was always a great deal of nautical interest to be seen during the run up Belfast Lough.

But this service was more than that. It provided the first reasonable facilities for steerage passengers on the Irish services from the Clyde, and it was also a quick way of reaching Dublin, Derry and other major destinations within the compass of a day's travel. It was no wonder that it was popular for almost 90 years.

All the early services between the Clyde and Ireland were operated overnight. The first attempt to run a daytime service was made in 1860 when G. & J. Burns took delivery of a very fine paddle steamer, to be capable of a speed of almost 20 knots. Named *Giraffe*, she made a trip with invited guests from Greenock to Belfast in 5 hours 45 minutes, and, leaving Belfast again at 4.00pm, her passengers were back in Glasgow at 11.35. The service ran during the Glasgow Fair holidays (the second fortnight of July), but it was found to be impossible for the ship to maintain the speed of her initial crossing and the service was not repeated in 1861. In 1862 *Giraffe* was sold to the Confederate States for a very satisfactory £30,000, to serve as a blockade runner.

Burns tried again in 1884 with a new twin-screw ship named *Buzzard*. The Scottish terminal was now Ardrossan and, leaving Glasgow St Enoch station at 7.45am and the port at 9.00am, arrival in Belfast was scheduled for 1.45pm, a crossing time of just over 5 hours. Even when arrival was punctual, there was little time for day excursionists to see much of the city since *Buzzard* set off again at 2.30pm, Ardrossan being reached at 8.30 and Glasgow at 10.08. The service was operated again in 1885 but clearly failed to attract sufficient numbers and was not repeated in 1886, the ship being sold to Greek owners in 1887.

The development of large paddle steamers, with promenade decks extending the full length of the vessel, by the Fairfield yard in the 1880s, beginning with *Victoria* for the London, Chatham & Dover Railway in 1886, no doubt encouraged Burns to try a daylight service again, using a ship of this type. Accordingly in 1889 the company took delivery of *Cobra* and instituted a service from the Caledonian Railway's new pier at Gourock. Referred to in press accounts as the 'new and magnificent ps *Cobra*', she was indeed a very fine vessel and was the first on any Irish service to be designed for passengers only, thus giving the designers plenty of scope in her internal layout. They took full advantage of this, the improvement being particularly marked in the steerage.

The promenade deck ran from stem to stern, allowing plenty of deck space for passengers in both classes. Below this, on the main deck forward, there was a large room for steerage passengers, completely enclosed against the elements. Passages ran from this on both side of the engine room to the 1st Class accommodation, allowing passengers to see something of the engines at work. The 1st Class saloon did not extend for the full width of the ship, since alleyways, open at the sides, ran to the stern, but it was lit by large square windows and, upholstered in crimson velvet, had a most attractive appearance. Forward of it there was a single stateroom and a cloakroom, and aft was a smoke room, panelled in oak and fitted with chairs and settees upholstered in brown leather. The dining saloon was on the

A view of *Cobra* lying off Heligoland after her sale to German owners. Apart from the awnings, she was unaltered from her days on the Clyde. *Author's collection*

lower deck and forward of it was a ladies' boudoir in walnut and satinwood, with old gold upholstery. Steerage dining facilities were located on the lower deck forward, in separate rooms for 'males and females'; presumably married couples had to split up to dine! Electric light was fitted throughout.

Despite her magnificence, *Cobra* had only one season on the daylight crossing. It is not clear if there were defects that came to light only after she had entered service, but she was returned to her builders in part-exchange for a new vessel, and was placed in service in North Wales, together with the ex-LB&SCR ship *Paris*. The ships were registered in the name of Richard Branwell, Managing Director of the shipyard. However, she remained there, as *Saint Tudno*, for only one year and was then sold to the firm of Albert Ballin of Hamburg for use on the service to Heligoland from that city and Cuxhaven. With her former name restored, she settled down at last and performed well on this service, with occasional winter trips to the Mediterranean for use between Genoa and the Riviera. She was allocated to France for reparations after 1918 but was bought back by what was now the Hamburg-Amerika Line and ran for two more seasons before being withdrawn in 1921. The Germans had become so fond of her that her name was perpetuated on a new turbine steamer of 1926.

To replace her Burns acquired virtually a repeat ship, *Adder*, which was slightly longer, of shallower draught and about 1 knot faster. Her departure point was changed to Greenock, but in 1892 it was moved to Ardrossan, where it remained for as long as the service operated. She seems to have been more satisfactory than her predecessor but was not so steady, having a reputation for pitching and rolling. After a few years her owners decided to give her a more suitable livery than their usual dismal all-over black, and she then had yellow funnels with black tops, a white saloon and white paddle boxes. She was clearly successful and latterly carried between 70,000 and 80,000 passengers each season When replaced in 1906, *Adder* was sold to Argentinian owners for service to Montevideo and, as *Rio de la Plata*, she continued on this until wrecked in 1918.

With the development of turbine machinery, Burns decided to order a replacement fitted with that type of propulsion and on 10 March 1906 Lady Inverclyde launched *Viper* from the Fairfield yard. She was to be one of the most handsome and successful steamers ever to sail on the Irish Sea. On the promenade (awning) deck were the saloon entrance, with purser's office, smoke room, tearoom and some private cabins. The 1st Class saloon and ladies' lounges were on the main deck forward, and the dining saloon was below these. This could accommodate 125 diners, who sat at tables for eight or six. Facilities for passengers in 2nd Class were on the main and lower decks aft, with a general saloon and ladies' room on the former and a dining saloon for 105 passengers – no longer segregated by gender – on the lower deck. Not only the quality of the fittings but also an increase in crew numbers to 80, from the 58 on *Adder*, showed the standard of service that her owners intended to offer to the 1,700 members of the travelling public. Writing in 1945, a former

A postcard sketch of *Adder* after the adoption of yellow funnels and white upperworks. *Author's collection*

regular traveller recalled with fondness the breakfasts of porridge and fresh cream, followed by grilled kippers, tea or coffee and toast, all for 2s 6d, and the dinners on the return sailing of soup, sole, lamb and Swiss tart or fruit and cream, at a cost of 4s 6d or 5 shillings.

On 15 May, a day of sun, showers and a fresh breeze, *Viper* made an inaugural cruise to Belfast, the white horses in the North Channel giving her a chance to demonstrate her excellent sea-going qualities. She made the passage in 3½ hours and on arrival at Albert Quay was thrown open to the public for inspection, an opportunity of which Belfast's citizens took full advantage. As one local

workman informed a reporter from Glasgow's *Evening Times*, 'Oi've been over the *Voiper*, had sangwidges and whiskey and all in me dinner time.' Having thus been admired, the ship settled down to her normal routine, under command of Captain MacLaren, a 'careful, courteous and affable officer'. A connecting train left Glasgow Central at 9.15am and arrival in Belfast was at 1.45pm. She left again at 4.00pm and passengers were back in Central at 9.22. The day return fare, 3rd Class and cabin, was 10 shillings, and a 14-day

Viper off Wemyss Bay on the Clyde, probably en route to her trials. *McLean Museum & Art Gallery, Inverclyde Council*

return was 13s 6d. A 3rd Class and steerage day return was also offered at 6 shillings. With more than 2 full hours ashore, the number of day excursionists increased considerably.

Although she had only eight years on the service, *Viper* became an institution on both sides of the North Channel. Residents around Belfast Lough found that they could set their clocks by her, and her rich and sonorous siren, which her captain did not hesitate to use, could be heard far and wide. In an interview, Captain MacLaren gave his view that the travelling public were now much better behaved than had been the case 20 years previously. They were not so 'uncouth', showed much more consideration for women and children, and did not jostle at the gangway.

A very successful troopship in the English Channel, *Viper* returned to her old haunts in 1919, and at the Glasgow Fair carried crowds. But Ireland was no longer a place to visit unless one had to, and in March 1920 she was sold to the Isle of Man Steam Packet Co, by whom she was renamed *Snaefell*. She made a useful member of that company's fleet, often operating from Fleetwood and re-visiting Ardrossan at holiday times. During the Second World War, she was one of the two ships that maintained the vital link with the island, from Fleetwood, and at the end of it she was so worn out that she was immediately sold, in August 1945, for breaking up at Port Glasgow.

Laird Line had for many years served Portrush, a resort that attracted many visitors from Scotland,

Above Late in her career and looking distinctly run-down, *Snaefell* leaves Fleetwood for Douglas during the Second World War. *National Maritime Museum*

Below The Isle of Man steamer *Snaefell* (1948) leaving Rothesay Pier in July 1960 on the return part of a day trip from Belfast. *Author*

by a twice-weekly overnight sailing. In 1892 this was changed to a daylight service, sailing from Gourock on alternate days, but in August a daily service was provided, using two ships. Some of the Laird ships were too large to enter Portrush harbour at that time, and passengers had to be landed by small boats. On Mondays the steamer called off Ballycastle, and on several days cruises were offered from Portrush once the cross-channel passengers had disembarked. These included around Rathlin, to Red Bay or to Moville, with a cruise on Lough Foyle. Passenger numbers increased in the early 1900s and it was decided that a day return service throughout the summer would be viable. In 1907 the company took delivery of *Hazel* for this purpose from the Fairfield yard.

On 11 June 1907 *Hazel* took a party of 250 invited guests on a cruise round Arran and obviously made a favourable impression. For passengers in 1st Class there was a dining saloon with 80 places, a separate tearoom, a ladies' cabin and a fruit and confectionery stall. The dining saloon was panelled in mahogany with a satinwood inlay and was ventilated by electric fans, with individual small tables being provided in place of the customary long tables. The tearoom was in oak with a tulipwood inlay, and the smoke room was also in oak with red marble tops to the tables. There was also a separate deck lounge. For those in 2nd Class there was a dining saloon and a ladies' saloon on the poop deck.

Clearly *Hazel* was ship built to a very high standard of comfort. The day of the cruise was fine, after rain in the morning, so *Hazel* had no chance to demonstrate her notorious propensity to roll, a feature that, for many passengers, would lessen her attraction. A shallow draught had been necessary to cope with the limitations of Portrush harbour and she carried a good deal of top hamper.

The journey was now via Ardrossan and the connecting train left Glasgow Central at 8.50am, giving an arrival in Portrush at 1.45pm; the actual crossing time was about 4½ hours. On the return journey she left at 3.45pm and passengers were in Glasgow just before 10. In 1913 more than 25,000 passengers used this service. The day or weekend

return fare in 1913 for 3rd Class rail and cabin was 11 shillings, a very reasonable amount when compared with contemporary fares on Clyde steamers.

Unfortunately there was now no time to offer local cruises from Portrush although they were operated occasionally from Rothesay, Ayr, Troon and Whiting Bay. In 1912 they operated from Rothesay on 15 July and 5 August, from Ayr on 17 July and 14 August, from Troon on 18 July, and from Whiting Bay on 16 and 29 July and 12 and 26 August. At other times through fares were offered from Arran piers, by Caledonian or Glasgow & South Western Railway steamer to Ardrossan. The service was duplicated on the Friday of Glasgow Fair, with an extra daylight sailing at 9.00am from Ardrossan and a night crossing at 10.00pm. The ship used for these was the elderly *Dunure*, whose facilities must have formed a contrast to those on board *Hazel*. The latter became a fleet messenger in the war, which she survived, but, no doubt because of the troubles in

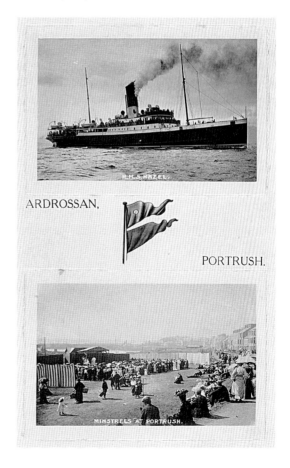

ARDROSSAN,

PORTRUSH.

A view of *Hazel* with the Laird line houseflag and a crowd enjoying the minstrels on the sands at Portrush. *Author's collection*

Ireland, the service was not resumed and she was sold to the Isle of Man SP Company. Re-named *Mona*, she was used on secondary services until scrapped in 1938.

The daylight service to Belfast was maintained in 1921/2 by *Graphic*, but she was too slow to give a reasonable time ashore and her facilities were those of a night service steamer. Thereafter the service went into a period of decline and it was not until 1933 that it was revived. In late 1932 Burns Laird bought the turbine steamer *Riviera* from the Southern Railway, reconditioned her and re-named her *Lairds Isle*. She was not quite so speedy as *Viper* had been, but she was still a fast ship and the day excursion traffic revived considerably. The day return fare from Glasgow was now 28 shillings, 3rd Class rail and saloon. All meals on board cost 2s 6d 1st Class and 2 shillings in what was now designated 'third saloon', and the quality of the catering was excellent.

Lairds Isle had a successful war career as successively an armed boarding vessel, a paravane ranging vessel, an infantry landing ship during the Normandy landings in June 1944, and a troop

Above *Lairds Isle* leaves Rothesay Bay on a misty Sunday morning after picking up excursion passengers for a cruise to Bangor or Larne. *Courtesy of National Museums Liverpool, Merseyside Maritime Museum*

Left A group of passengers on *Lairds Isle*: it is clearly a wet day and they do not seem to be enjoying the crossing. *G. E. Langmuir collection, the Mitchell Library, Glasgow City Council*

This leaflet containing the bar tariff from *Irish Coast* during 1958, her first summer of the daylight service, shows her sailing across a moonlit sea! A bottle of beer cost 1s 4d and a nip of whisky could be had for 2s 3d. *Author's collection*

carrier. She seemed to be a lucky ship during the war, surviving three collisions and the explosion of an acoustic mine. At the end of hostilities she was reconditioned to a much higher standard than before. The upper deck was extended aft, the dining saloon was relocated on the promenade deck, the forward portion of which was enclosed, and new lifeboats were fitted. She re-entered service on 29 July 1946 and continued until a somewhat abrupt withdrawal in August 1957. She had made the route as popular as *Viper* had done, and in post-war years, with rationing continuing in Britain, it also became a favourite route for smuggling. On one return crossing, a passenger in the ladies' cabin, of somewhat stout appearance, was observed to remove most of her outer garments – to the surprise of the others – then to unwrap from around her person a fine rug that she had bought in Dublin and had thus managed to import right under the eagle eyes of the Belfast customs men!

Irish Coast and, from 1965, *Scottish Coast* were used on the crossing thereafter, but, although both were fine ships, neither was really suited to a day service. Seating accommodation was limited and, although cabins were available, these were not laid out for those who wanted, perhaps, somewhere to sit and read, being basically only bedrooms. Their speed was also limited and only an hour was now offered ashore for day trippers. It was not until the car ferry *Lion* was commissioned in January 1968 that the daylight crossing once again had a ship designed to meet its needs.

These were the regular services, but at times other ships gave day excursions in both directions across the North Channel. As an example, Burns's *Partridge* gave a day excursion to Campbeltown from Belfast on 24 August 1907, leaving at 8.00am and returning from Kintyre at 5.00pm. For this she was operated as a one-class ship and, at 3s 6d

return, this was clearly something of a bargain. For an additional shilling, excursionists could take a trip to Machrihanish on the light railway, and that company laid on a special express train in connection with the sailing. *Lairds Isle* made regular Sunday trips in the 1930s; on 25 June 1933 she sailed form Ardrossan (10.15am) and Ayr to Bangor, where excursionists had almost 4 hours ashore before returning at 5.00pm, while on 16 July – despite a hectic schedule over the Friday and Saturday – she gave a coastal cruise to Rathlin and the Giant's Causeway, leaving at 10.15am and returning to Ardrossan at 8.00pm. A train was run from Glasgow to connect with these cruises, and in both cases the fare was 11 shillings. On other days she started form Rothesay, usually at 8.30am. Day trips from Ireland were latterly run almost exclusively by the ships of the Isle of Man Steam Packet Co, the usual destination being Rothesay, but with the decline of the classic passenger ships, these too came to an end.

4. HANDLING THE PEAK: GLASGOW FAIR HOLIDAY TRAFFIC

The Glasgow Fair holiday is of ancient origin and at first was simply a holiday of a day or two when a fair was held on Glasgow Green. By the 20th century this had evolved into a fortnight, the last two weeks of July, when all factories and shipyards closed down and the workers went on holiday out of the city. With holidays with pay being common from about 1930 onwards, more and more people took the opportunity to travel. As many of those working in heavy industry and labouring jobs in the West of Scotland were of Irish origin, they naturally wanted to use this holiday to visit the folks back home. By this time too, middle-class Glasgow was becoming more

Lairdsbank (the former *Olive*) takes a holiday sailing from Glasgow in July 1930, with a good crowd of steerage passengers on board. *G. E. Langmuir collection, the Mitchell Library, Glasgow City Council*

adventurous in its choice of holiday destinations, and Irish resorts such as Portrush and Newcastle (Co Down) were beginning to attract quite a following.

From the point of view of shipping operators, the trouble with all these people was that they all wanted to travel outwards at more or less the same time. In some years the Glasgow holidays coincided with the Belfast holidays around 12 July, which provided a certain amount of return traffic, together with those returning from a holiday in the first fortnight, but on the whole the workings were very unbalanced. The return peak at the end of July was not quite so concentrated, as some would have taken only a week's break and some families would stay on in Ireland while only the breadwinner came back to Glasgow.

Ireland was not, of course, the only holiday destination favoured by Glaswegians. The Isle of

Rose **leaves Ardrossan on a holiday sailing. She is still carrying Laird Line colours, but the date is unknown.** *G. E. Langmuir collection, the Mitchell Library, Glasgow City Council*

Man had a loyal following among both working- and middle-class people. The problem for the Isle of Man company was that some of the Lancashire 'Wakes Weeks' would coincide with the Fair and stretch its fleet's capacity to the full. Its services and many of the extra services to Ireland were worked through Ardrossan, which was of course also the starting point for steamers to Arran, another middle-class favourite. Air services to both Ireland and the Isle of Man were in operation by 1939, but as yet they took only a tiny fraction of the traffic, most of which still went by sea. This chapter looks at how the companies involved tried to cope with this annual movement when it was at its peak.

The holidays normally began at lunchtime on the Friday and no doubt many of those thus released would have spent a little time celebrating before they returned home to pick up the family and head off for the Broomielaw, Central or St Enoch stations. Harassed staff then had the additional problem of coping with those who had no very clear idea of which ship was which or what they had done with the tickets or what was their actual destination, and it was a tribute to the staff's resourcefulness that most travellers ended up on the right boat or train when departure time came. Burns and Laird Lines issued a special timetable leaflet each year to make it all quite simple.

In 1939 the mass exodus actually began on the night of Thursday 13 July, when two or, if required, three overnight sailings to Belfast were laid on via Ardrossan, all departing at 8.00pm. The first two were taken by *Lairdshill* and *Louth*, the latter chartered from the British & Irish Steam Packet Co, and, as *Graphic*, no stranger to Ardrossan. If required, the Dublin ship *Lairdsburn* would give the third sailing. The same pattern was repeated on the Friday night, but with *Lairdshill* and *Lairdsburn* leaving at 9.00pm and *Lairds Isle* following an hour later, and no doubt passing the first two en route. At this stage in her carer, *Lairdshill* could just about manage 14 knots, but by post-war years this had come down to about 12 knots with a following wind – she was no greyhound! From the point of view of those in 1st

The lifeboats on *Lairds Isle* have been swung out, not in anticipation of an imminent submarine attack but simply to make more room on the upper deck on a busy crossing, probably during the Glasgow Fair holidays. *G. E. Langmuir collection, the Mitchell Library, Glasgow City Council*

Class, there was no problem if they had succeeded in obtaining a cabin, but if they had not been so lucky there would have been difficulty finding a seat under cover; the lounge on *Lairdshill* would have taken, at most, 50 people.

On *Lairds Isle* the problem was reversed. She had ample seating accommodation, but only a few cabins. Perhaps this did not actually matter too much, as passengers were turned off when she reached Belfast in the small hours, to allow her to dash back to Ardrossan for her normal morning departure, leaving them to sit, surrounded by tired children and piles of luggage, in the unwelcoming sheds of Donegall Quay until the trains and trams

started running in about 3 hours. If the weather was fine, it was an uncomfortable night for many; if the sea was rough it was unbelievably awful. On Saturday the 15th, *Lairds Isle* took her normal morning sailing and stragglers were catered for by sailings of *Louth* and *Lairdshill*, both at 11.30pm.

Meanwhile, back in Glasgow, the normal sailings of *Royal Ulsterman* and *Royal Scotsman* at 10.00pm on the Friday and Saturday respectively were duplicated by *Lairdscastle* at the same time on

A busy scene at Glasgow on Saturday 16 July 1960, with the two 'Royal' sisters, not often seen together, a cargo vessel and, beyond her, **Scottish Coast**. *Electric Railway Society*

the Friday and by *Lairdsgrove* at 11.00pm on the Saturday. A service to Dublin was given on each of the three nights concerned. On the Thursday the chartered *Ulster Prince* of the Belfast SS Company gave passengers a very comfortable night's travel, while on the Friday and Saturday *Lady Connaught* was on the service, leaving at 5.15 and 9.00pm respectively.

Many Glasgow Irish people came from Donegal and the normal thrice-weekly service to Derry operated in duplicate on both Thursday 13 and Friday 14 July. On the former, *Lairdsgrove* left at 5.00pm to relieve the normal sailing of *Lairdsglen* at 6.00pm, and on the Friday both these ships left at 6.00pm, having been preceded by *Lairdsrose* at 5.

The pattern of sailings at Stranraer seems to have been less organised, with ships sailing as often as they could to clear the crowds. On Fair Saturday 1937 seven crossings were made by *Princess Margaret* and *Princess Maud*. The main problem for the Stranraer route was not the sea passage – even if the ship was crowded, it was only a 2-hour sail – but the working of relief trains, often made up to 15 coaches, mainly of non-corridor stock, over the single-line railway from Girvan. If the overnight train from London arrived late on the Saturday morning, which it seems often to have done at holiday periods, the whole day was affected. On the Irish side, the opening of the new track layout at Greenisland in 1934 allowed the operation of through trains from Larne to Portrush. If the NCC was also operating relief trains to cover Irish holidays, this could have a knock-on effect on the boat trains at Larne.

For the Isle of Man, three sailings were normally given from Ardrossan (Montgomerie Pier) on Fair Friday, at 12 midday, 5.00pm and 11.30pm. The crossing took about 5½ hours and Douglas landladies were not always welcoming to those who arrived about midnight or first thing in the morning. There were corresponding return workings from Douglas, some of which called at Ramsey.

Cabin reservations had to be made with the steward on board, but most passengers had to sit up all night on the 11.30pm sailing, 1st and 2nd Class alike. On a good day, a daylight sailing provided a very scenic trip, as the ship was seldom out of sight of land and the coastal scenery was fine.

Against the background of the Arran mountains, the magnificent **Lady of Mann** of 1930 approaches Ardrossan on Friday 28 July 1967. *Author*

The Manx company's *Mona's Isle* of 1951 alongside Montgomerie Pier on 28 July 1967. *Author*

It should be remembered that, as far as Ardrossan was concerned, this peak traffic also involved the running of many extra trains, usually via the former Caledonian Railway line from Glasgow Central, and managers must have blessed the competition of the 1890s that had given rise to the duplication of lines, making this level of service possible. In 1938, in connection with Fair holiday sailings, five trains were run from Central to Ardrossan Montgomerie Pier between 7.25 and 8.40pm on Thursday 14 July. On the Friday there were seven between 6.55 and

8.40pm, and on the Saturday five between 7.20 and 8.40pm. Rather later there would have been several trains bringing passengers to the Isle of Man steamer. All these were made up of anything up to ten non-corridor carriages and, as the pier station had only two roads, some quick shunting must have taken place to allow following trains access to a platform. Nor were there many facilities for passengers from earlier trains waiting to board their ship, but no doubt some found consolation in one or other of Ardrossan's hostelries.

5. 'THE CLYDEWAY IS THE BEST WAY'

Thus for many years ran the advertising slogan used by the Burns & Laird Lines to popularise its services from the Clyde.

The Glasgow-Belfast service was probably the oldest cross-channel service to be worked on a regular basis, since the first crossings were made in

One of the most successful and long-serving steamers of the Burns fleet was *Vulture*, built by A. & J. Inglis in 1898. Originally she served the Ardrossan route, but was transferred to the Glasgow service in 1906 and remained there for many years, apart from a brief period of war service as a transport in the North Sea. She was modernised and converted to oil fuel in 1924, and in 1930 went back to Ardrossan, now named *Lairdsrock*. She remained on that route until it closed in August 1936. She was then sold to David MacBrayne and became the cruise ship *Lochgarry*. In this guise she was also very popular, but war intervened and, while serving as a troopship on the Iceland run, she was lost in 1941. The illustration shows her on the Clyde in Burns's colours and obviously before conversion to oil fuel! *McLean Museum & Art Gallery, Inverclyde Council*

the summer of 1818, and it continued from then – initially with breaks during the winter – until 1968. A service to Dublin was started in the summer of 1823, and at about the same time steamers began to serve Derry from the Clyde, these workings being at first an extension of excursion sailings to the Giant's Causeway. Ultimately the traffic was concentrated in the hands of G. & J. Burns Ltd and Laird Line Ltd, between whom there was peaceful co-existence rather than outright competition. These firms were amalgamated under Coast Lines management in 1922 and became Burns & Laird Lines Ltd.

The premier passenger route was Glasgow to Belfast, but until 1936 there was also a nightly service from Ardrossan to Belfast. In the early days there was not a great deal of cabin traffic, since tourism had not developed and passengers were mainly businessmen or commercial travellers. For

them, in ships such as *Thistle* of 1882, there was a dining saloon with 34 places forward on the promenade deck, this also providing sleeping accommodation with 14 berths. There were also seven two-berth cabins and a small smoke room on the upper deck. Washbasins were shared between adjoining cabins. For steerage passengers, of whom there were several hundred, there was nothing at all.

Facilities were greatly improved in 1930 when two ships were transferred from the British & Irish Steam Packet Company to become *Lairdsburn* and *Lairdscastle*. In turn these were replaced in 1936 by two magnificent new motorships of what was by now the standard Harland & Wolff design, *Royal*

Ulsterman and *Royal Scotsman*. These were based closely on the design of *Ulster Monarch*, but had only a single funnel and the interior furnishing and decoration was much more contemporary, being carried out in a restrained Art Deco style. They were attractively furnished and the fine woodwork was particularly remarked upon. They were extremely comfortable ships and the improvement in 3rd Class was most marked, since passengers there could now enjoy the luxury of a berth in a two-berth cabin and had their own dining saloon, smoke room and lounge. The pair maintained the service almost to the end and were withdrawn in 1967 and 1968 respectively.

Vulture's sister ship was *Magpie* and she had a broadly similar career until 1906, when she was transferred to the Derry service until 1908. She then ran to Dublin as an express boat until 1911, when she was given portable dining saloons for use on excursion trips. In 1929 she became *Lairdsgrove* and became a fixture on the Derry service, latterly without passenger accommodation. She was sold for scrapping in 1948. She is seen here at Ardrossan Winton Pier. *Andrew McQueen collection, Glasgow University Archives*

Redbreast was a single ship built for the Glasgow-Belfast service by Harland & Wolff Ltd at its Govan yard in 1908 and was the last of the traditional Burns design. During the First World War she became a decoy ship and was sunk in 1917. *Glasgow University Archives*

Above Before the new ships arrived, Burns Laird borrowed the City of Cork Company's motorship *Innisfallen* for a few weeks in early 1936, to familiarise crews and staff with the handling of a large motorship. She was a smaller edition of the 'Ulster' ships, built in 1930. Her funnels were repainted red and in this guise she is seen at Glasgow. *G. E. Langmuir collection, the Mitchell Library, Glasgow City Council*

Below On the Clyde, the Belfast steamers originally sailed from Anderston Quay in Glasgow, downstream from the berths used by the Clyde steamers. When these moved across the river to Bridge Wharf in 1929, only the ships of the Campbeltown Company remained to share the wharf, and these were withdrawn in 1940. The large sheds at the wharf were unwelcoming, to say the least, and in 1953 a new terminal was opened at Lancefield Quay, about half a mile down river. This offered a much higher standard of comfort and comprised a waiting room with seating, a baggage office and a ticket office. It was also open to passengers bound for Derry and Dublin, although their ships did not sail from there. In the first picture, the elderly *Davaar* of the Campbeltown company makes an interesting comparison with the nearer *Royal Scotsman*. *Author's collection*

Top At Donegall Quay, Belfast, on 14 December 1959 are (nearest the camera) *Royal Scotsman*, with ahead of her *Duke of Argyll, Slieve Bearnagh* and *Ulster Prince*. *Author*

Above By 9 March 1979 the only occupant was the freight ferry *Dalriada*. *Author*

Left Lancefield Quay, the successor to Glasgow's Anderston Quay, is seen in December 1964. *Royal Ulsterman* takes on fuel from a small tanker named *Calamity*. *Author*

Services to Derry

An exterior view of the new terminal at Lancefield Quay, from a publicity leaflet. *Author's collection*

Services from the Clyde to Derry were largely a Laird Line preserve, with Burns operating only once a week. By 1905 there were sailings by the former on Monday, Tuesday, Thursday and Friday, leaving Glasgow at midday but with a train connection at Greenock at 3.00pm. Fares in 1st Class were 12s 6d single and 17s 6d return, and steerage was 4 shillings single only; returns were available on Burns's sailings. By now tourist traffic was developing and through bookings were available to Bundoran, Enniskillen and Sligo via the Great Northern and the Sligo, Leitrim & Northern Counties trains. A 14-day return from Glasgow to Bundoran, 3rd rail and cabin on the ship, cost 22s 6d. Similar fares were available for travel on the narrow gauge trains of the Londonderry & Lough Swilly Railway to the resorts it served, Buncrana and Burtonport.

Lairdsgrove (formerly *Magpie*) was regularly on the Derry service in the 1930s and is seen here leaving Glasgow in June 1933. She did not carry passengers after 1939 and was broken up in 1948. *Author's collection*

Latterly Derry was served by *Lairdsloch*, the only cross-channel ship to be built during the Second World War (1944), though as a cargo vessel only at the time. Her construction emphasises the importance of the livestock trade, even in the middle of a war. Passenger accommodation was added in 1946, though in the case of steerage this did not amount to much of an alteration! Apart from a small refreshment room, in summer steerage consisted of rows of hard seating in the area occupied at other times by livestock. There were no berths of any sort for 3rd Class passengers. The 1954 timetable mentioned her very comfortable public rooms and the single- and two-berth cabins, but did not add that these were in 1st Class only! After closure of the Derry service in 1966, she made some runs to Belfast before being sold to Israeli owners. She was damaged by a mine in 1970 and became a total loss.

By 1954 the frequency was three times per week in summer and twice in winter, and the crossing took exactly 12 hours. A train connection via Greenock was still offered on Fridays, apart from Glasgow Fair Friday. Fares from Glasgow were now 43s 5d or 22s 7d single and 72s 4d and 45s 2d return, 1st and steerage respectively.

BURNS & LAIRD LINES, LTD.

LOUGH SWILLY BUS SERVICES.

THROUGH TICKETS FROM GLASGOW TO PLACES IN CO. DONEGAL

During summer season **1958**, through Return Tickets can be obtained from Burns & Laird Lines, Ltd., Glasgow, Greenock and Edinburgh offices, by direct steamer via Londonderry to places in Co. Donegal served by the "Lough Swilly" Bus Services.

The following is a list of the principal places served :—

ANNAGRY	GWEEDORE
BUNCRANA	GREENCASTLE
BALLYLIFFIN	GORTAHORK
BURTONPORT	KERRYKEEL
BUNBEG	KINCASSLAGH
CULDAFF	LETTERKENNY
CLONMANY	MOVILLE
CARNDONAGH	MALIN HEAD
CARRIGART	MALIN TOWN
CREESLOUGH	MILFORD
DOWNINGS	MEENALECK
DUNFANAGHY	PORTSALON
DUNGLOE	PORTNABLAGH
DERRYBEG	QUIGLEY'S POINT
FALCARRAGH	RAMELTON
FAHAN	RATHMULLAN
	(via Letterkenny)

"Lough Swilly" Buses meet Steamers on arrival at Londonderry during "Fair" and other peak periods.
Private parties specially catered for.
Particulars on application to :—
BURNS & LAIRD LINES, LTD.,
52 ROBERTSON STREET, GLASGOW, C.2,
or
LOUGH SWILLY RAILWAY, LONDONDERRY.

Above *Lairdsbank*, see here on Lough Foyle, was built as one of a trio in 1936 and spent most of her working life on the former Laird Line's Heysham-Derry service. She could carry about 300 cattle, as well as horses and sheep. The spaces occupied by the animals were ventilated by fans, to a level well above statutory requirements. She took the last Heysham-Derry sailing on 12 October 1963 and was then transferred to the B&I Company for service from Cork. *G. E. Langmuir collection, the Mitchell Library, Glasgow City Council*

Above right A 1958 Burns & Laird handbill. *Author's collection*

Below *Lairdsloch* at Princes Quay, Derry, on 1 August 1964. *Author*

From the Clyde to Dublin

Glasgow and the Irish capital were first connected by steamer in 1826, a link that was to be maintained for the next 142 years. At the beginning of the period under review, the service was provided on four days per week in each direction by the ships of the Dublin & Glasgow Sailing & Steam Packet Company, a firm that remained wedded to the paddle steamer for some time after other companies had gone over to screw propulsion. Advertisements stated that the ships were at liberty to take a tow and to sail with or without pilots.

In its steamers, cabin passengers had a combined dining and sitting saloon on deck and sleeping accommodation was on the lower deck, total accommodation being for about 100. Steerage passengers were carried on deck forward. Perhaps making a virtue out of necessity, advertisements enthused about the almost total absence of vibration and stated also that the accommodation was thoroughly well ventilated.

Through trains in connection with its steamers were operated from Edinburgh to Greenock by the North British and G&SWR companies. The last paddler, and the last ship of this type to be built for night service from the Clyde, was *Duke of Argyll*, built by R. Duncan of Port Glasgow in 1873. She lasted until 1905. Originally fitted with two-cylinder simple oscillating engines, she was given new compound oscillating engines and new boilers by A. & J. Inglis in 1881.

The congestion on the Liffey in the 19th century has been mentioned elsewhere, but the LNWR was not the only shipping company to be affected by it. On 22 October 1883 *Duke of Leinster* sank off Pigeon House after colliding with the wreck of a dredger that had in turn been sunk by a collier. No lives were lost and the ship was later raised and returned to service.

Possibly because the Glasgow agent was heavily involved with the City Bank of Glasgow, which spectacularly failed in 1878, there was then a hiatus in the acquisition of new ships, but the first screw steamer, *General Gordon*, appeared in 1885, and between 1892 and 1906 the company placed three very fine ships in service. All bore the names of Dukes, of Fife, Rothesay and Montrose, and *General Gordon* was in 1895 renamed *Duke of Gordon* to bring her into line. The company often traded as the Duke Line.

The Laird Line also traded between Glasgow and Dublin, but usually in co-operation with the D&G, rather than in opposition to it, to provide a service on six days a week from 1880 onwards. The latter fleet was taken over by Burns in 1908, Lord Inverclyde, the Chairman of that company, being concerned about competition with the route via his steamers and Belfast.

Fares in 1878 were 15 shillings single, 22s 6d return in cabin, and 6 and 10 shillings in steerage.

Duke of Leinster alongside at an unknown location. *G. E. Langmuir collection, the Mitchell Library, Glasgow City Council*

Duke of Rothesay **on the Clyde.** *Glasgow University Archives*

From New Year's Day 1909 departure from Glasgow, hitherto variable, was fixed at 2.00pm and from Greenock Princes Pier, via connecting train, at 6.30pm. The time of the passage from Glasgow was about 18 hours.

Burns also instituted a once-weekly express sailing, generally worked by *Magpie*, which did not leave Glasgow until 8.00pm. Laird Line fares in 1912 were 14 and 22 shillings cabin and 6s 6d and 10s 6d in steerage.

By 1920 facilities had greatly improved, especially for passengers in steerage, for whom sleeping accommodation was first provided in *Ermine*, built in 1912 by Fairfield, but based very closely on the 'Duke' ships. The Burns guide mentions that breakfast, lunch and tea were obtainable for 3s 6d in cabin and 2s 6d in steerage, while in the former dinner was provided at 6 shillings. There was now a separate charge of 2s 6d for a berth in a two- or four-berth cabin and any servants travelling cabin had to pay full fare.

Passengers were no doubt re-assured to know that the bed linen was changed daily, presumably in contrast to former practice! Their boots would be cleaned for them if they left them outside the cabin door, but they were warned to examine there carefully when returned in the morning, to avoid any confusion. They were also warned to keep portholes closed in wet weather. Stewardesses would enter only the ladies' cabin or a lady's stateroom.

The facilities on this route were greatly improved in 1936 when the two ships that had been maintaining the Belfast service from Glasgow were transferred to it on the arrival of the new motorships. These were *Lairdsburn* and *Lairdscastle*, originally built in 1923 for the British & Irish Steam Packet Company's service between Liverpool and Dublin, as *Lady Louth* and *Lady Limerick* respectively. With berths for 80 saloon

Lairdshill **shares North Wall with the LMS cargo steamer** *Slieve More* **in October 1947.** *G. E. Langmuir collection, the Mitchell Library, Glasgow City Council*

The upper reaches of the Liffey were still quite congested with shipping in June 1965. *Irish Coast* awaits her next departure to Glasgow at the North Wall. The collier *Warwickbrook* of the Williamstown Shipping Co of London is at the quay on the left, while *Granouaille*, one of the vessels of the Commissioners of Irish Lights, heads upstream and a small cargo ship makes for the sea. *Author*

and 90 steerage passengers, they were comfortable and very steady ships. 1st Class accommodation was on the main, promenade and upper decks, and, apart from cabins, there was an attractive dining saloon, with tables for four, on the promenade deck, and a lounge forward on the upper deck. Steerage passengers were accommodated in the poop. The two ships returned to the Belfast service during the Second World War and, while so engaged, *Lairdscastle* was sunk off Corsewall Point

after a collision on 4 September 1940. Her sister survived until 1953, by which time sailings had been reduced to three per week.

Lairdscastle was replaced, on summer sailings, by Coast Lines' newest and very luxurious motorship *Irish Coast*, built by Harland & Wolff of Belfast. When she went off to take over the daylight sailings, she was replaced by her near-sister *Scottish Coast* of 1957. Both ships brought superb facilities to this service, but they really came too late in the day, as airlines were now taking most of the regular traffic and the ships were full only at peak holiday times. Even on those occasions, air began to make inroads in the 1960s and, when both ships were required for the Liverpool-Belfast route in the autumn of 1966, the Dublin service finally closed after 143 years.

		1st class			3rd class	
To	Single	Return	Excursion return	Single	Return	Excursion return
1938						
Belfast	20s	32s	20s 9d	9s 6d	19s	12s 9d
Derry	20s	32s	20s 9d	9s 6d	19s	12s 9d
Dublin	21s	35s 6d	28s 9d	11s	22s	14s 9d
1954						
Belfast	47s 10d	82s 3d	N/A	21s 8d	39s	N/A
Derry	43s 5d	72s 4d	N/A	22s 7d	45s 2d	N/A
Dublin	45s 3d	78s 7d	N/A	25s 3d	50s 6d	N/A

Glasgow-Ireland fares in 1938 and 1954

Cargo ships

Although they attracted less notice than the passenger ships, the cargo vessels were probably more important to the company, in terms of earnings. As with the railway ships, much of this earning power came from the transport of cattle and other livestock.

Top   The second *Lairdscastle* was a standard ship of the First World War, which came to Burns Laird in 1948 after a very varied career, which had included temporary wartime service with the company from 1941 to 1946. She was used entirely as a cattle ship and was withdrawn in 1957, just after this picture was taken. G. A. Osbon, *courtesy of the World Ship Society*

Middle   When the new motorships appeared in 1936 and the overnight Ardrossan to Belfast sailings were withdrawn, a new purely cargo service was started on a triangular Ardrossan-Belfast-Ayr route. Two new motorships were built for this by Harland & Wolff in Belfast, one of which was *Lairdscrest*. They could carry 295 cattle and six horses and had a general cargo capacity of 73,558cu ft. The animals' spaces were mechanically ventilated. A third identical ship, *Lairdsbank*, was built at the same time for the Heysham-Derry service. *Lairdscrest* is seen here at Glasgow in August 1964. She was sold to Panamanian owners in 1968 and scrapped ten years later. *Electric Railway Society*

Bottom   Completed in 1954 by the Ardrossan Dockyard Company, *Lairdsglen* was in the event the last cargo ship built for the company, though no one would have expected this at the time – Burns & Laird had always been part of the Clyde scene and always would be! With five goalpost masts, she was no beauty, but, as built, she had room for 480 head of cattle in addition to 750 tons of general cargo. She had been designed for possible conversion to a passenger/cargo ship, but with changing patterns of trade there was no call for this, and in 1969 she was altered instead to become a purely cattle carrier. As such she made several trips well beyond the British Isles and even reached Texas. In 1974 she was sold, and ended her days in Cartagena in late 1983. Taken in June 1957, this view shows her as built. G. A. Osbon, *courtesy of the World Ship Society*

6. NEW WINE INTO OLD BOTTLES

The British & Irish Steam Packet Company had quite a long history, but until 1920 it was overshadowed by the City of Dublin Company. It had provided a network of services linking Dublin and London with Falmouth, Plymouth, Portsmouth and Southampton, and even in pre-1914 days advertised rates for motor cars. Its ships were generally named after titled ladies.

Carlow was one of a series of ships built for the City Company for its Liverpool-Dublin service, a route always over-shadowed by the mail service. Before 1914 two services were provided daily and, as passengers on the night service were allowed to remain in their cabins until 9.00am, it would seem to have been a more civilised way of crossing to Ireland than the mail service, with its change from train to ship in the small hours! She was built at Port Glasgow in 1896 and passed to the B&I Company in 1919, being given the 'Lady' prefix to her name, and was broken up in 1925. In this view she shares a Liverpool landing stage with the famous paddle steamer *La Marguerite*. *Courtesy of National Museums Liverpool, Merseyside Maritime Museum*

The company took over four ex-City Company ships in 1919, together with the Liverpool-Dublin passenger service on which they had sailed. However, it was soon realised that something bigger and better would be required, and in 1923/4 two fine new ships entered service, *Lady Louth* and *Lady Limerick*. As a nightly service actually required three ships, the fairly new *Ardmore*, renamed *Lady Longford*, was transferred from the City of Cork SP Company. The trio built up a very good passenger base in the 1920s, as the service allowed travellers to have a full night's sleep, unlike that of the 'Irish Mail', and it was in any case slightly cheaper. It was therefore something of a shock to patrons when in 1929/30 the ships were transferred to Burns & Laird Lines and were replaced by the now-redundant Belfast steamers, *Graphic*, *Heroic* and *Patriotic*, for a cost of £25,000 for the first two and £35,000 for the last. These now became *Lady Munster*, *Lady Connaught* and

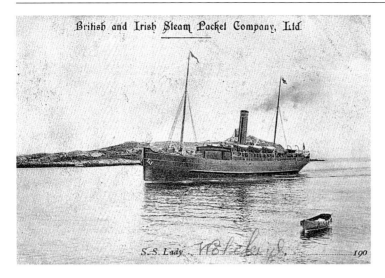

British and Irish Steam Packet Company, Ltd.

S.S. Lady *Wolseley* 190

Left It is not clear which B&I ship this actually is, but the card was posted at Plymouth on 26 March 1907 by a passenger on *Lady Wolseley*, a ship built at Barrow in 1894 and lost in 1915. *Author's collection*

Below Another of the 'Ladies' was *Lady Wimborne*, wife of the most ineffective of the later Lords Lieutenant. She was launched at Port Glasgow in 1915, the year in which this photograph was taken and the year in which he assumed the role, but fortunately she proved to have rather more staying power than he did – he was removed in 1916 – and was used on the Dublin-London service until 1935. *Glasgow University Archives*

Below In August 1922 the B&I Company acquired a ship that had become famous during the recent war. *Brussels* had been built for the Great Eastern Railway in 1902 and continued to run on North Sea passenger service during the war. Her master, Captain Charles Fryatt, became well-known for the cheeky challenges he mounted to German U-boats, one of which ultimately captured the vessel, on 23 June 1916. He was then tried and executed, thus becoming something of a martyr. After the war *Brussels* returned to Britain and was bought by a new company, the Dublin & Lancashire Shipping Company, for use in the Irish Sea cattle trade from Preston to Dublin. The new company was not welcomed by the B&I and, after a brief war, it sold out to the latter, which soon renamed the ship *Lady Brussels*. She continued to work on the Preston service for her new owners until 1929. The location of this view is not certain but it is probably Heysham. *Author's collection*

STATEROOM S. S. 'LADY LIMERICK' 1945 TONS.

B. & I. LINE
LIVERPOOL AND DUBLIN
NIGHTLY EXPRESS SERVICE (SUNDAYS EXCEPTED).

Left Lady Louth on the Clyde in July 1923. *Glasgow University Archives*

Left and above Views of the lounge and a single-berth cabin aboard Lady Limerick. *Author's collection*

LOUNGE S. S. "LADY LIMERICK" 1945 TONS.
B. & I. LINE. LIVERPOOL AND DUBLIN NIGHTLY EXPRESS SERVICE (SUNDAYS EXCEPTED).

Lady Connaught with the attractive but somewhat impractical grey hull. *Author's collection*

Lady Leinster. To make them look a bit more up-to-date, they were given two funnels of the motorship type then fashionable, but these sat ill on the long slim hulls, and the elegant counter sterns showed their true age. The poop decks were extended to the sterns, but otherwise the ships were not altered, and the lack of hot water in the cabins contrasted unfavourably with the new ships on the Belfast route. Like these they initially had grey hulls but these were soon repainted black.

Nonetheless, the three sisters worked well enough. In 1935/6 there were negotiations with the government of what was still the Irish Free State with a view to it acquiring a controlling interest in the line, and for a short period it was actually marketed as the 'Irish Free State Line'. However, these talks failed and it was to be another 30 years before the government of Ireland acquired the company. In the meantime, an improved financial position at last allowed it to order two new ships for the Dublin service in late 1936. With *Leinster* and *Munster*, the company more than made up for having inflicted elderly second-hand tonnage on Dublin passengers for the previous seven years. They came into service in

1937 and 1938 respectively and internally marked a complete break with both the old-fashioned seafaring tradition and also the Olde English country house style of the 'Ulster' trio. Their design represented all that was best in Art Deco, and a particular novelty was the fitting of fluorescent lighting in some of the public spaces. Much use was made of contrasting woods in the panelling; the restaurant was finished in oak relieved by walnut and sycamore, the whole being set off by blue chairs and curtains, and a floral-pattern carpet. Mirrors in the after bulkhead created an impression of even greater space, and these were emphasised by contrasting marquetry work. The lounge was in pine and had gold damask curtains, and the staircase to the boat deck actually came out in the middle of the smoke room, where a glass screen with doors gave access to the deck. Externally too there was a change, as the sisters had buff hulls, with green boot topping.

Sadly, Dublin passengers did not enjoy those fine vessels for long. *Munster* was lost after striking a magnetic mine while on the Belfast-Liverpool service on 6 February 1940, fortunately without any loss of life. After war service, *Leinster* was assigned to the Belfast SS Company and became *Ulster Prince*, making her first sailing on 28 February 1946. She lasted with the BSSC until

Right An advertisement for the service during the period when it was trading as Irish Free State Lines. Motor cars had begun to form an important part of the traffic. By the time the new ships entered service, the name had reverted to the former style, but the vintage car was still being slung aboard and somewhat spoiled the note of modernity. *Author's collection*

IRISH FREE STATE LINES

EXPRESS SERVICE EVERY WEEKDAY

LIVERPOOL & DUBLIN

DEPART LIVERPOOL 10.15 P.M.
DEPART DUBLIN
8.30 P.M. · SATURDAYS 11.0 P.M.

FREIGHT RATES
— ON —
MOTOR CARS
LIVERPOOL
AND DUBLIN

Single Rates at Owners' Risk.
Cars not exceeding 10 cwts.
Cars not exceeding 10 cwts. to 15 cwts.
Cars not exceeding 15 cwts. to 20 cwts.
Cars exceeding over 20 cwts.
Plus Liverpool Inwards Ports Dues and Customs Clearance Charges 6/3.

Return Rates at Owners' Risk when TWO or more passengers accompany the car.
Cars not exceeding 10 cwts.
Cars not exceeding 10 cwts. to 15 cwts.
Cars not exceeding 15 cwts. to 20 cwts.
Cars exceeding over 20 cwts.
Plus Customs Clearance Charge 5/- in each direction when accompanied by triptyque.

LIFTING GEAR APPROVED BY AUTOMOBILE ASSOCIATION

THE FLEET

s.s. " LADY LEINSTER "		2,253 tons
s.s. " LADY MUNSTER "		1,915 tons
s.s. " LADY CONNAUGHT "		1,912 tons

or Other Steamer.

Below A coloured postcard view of **Munster**. *Author's collection*

Motor Vessel " MUNSTER " (4,300 *tons*)
LIVERPOOL–DUBLIN EXPRESS SERVICE
BRITISH & IRISH STEAM PACKET CO., LTD.

Above *Munster* of 1948 at North Wall in June 1965. *Author*

Left The 3rd Class dormitory of *Innisfallen*, built by Denny for the Fishguard-Cork service in 1949, gives an idea of the facilities offered to those passengers. It is a great improvement on what was once available, but still somewhat cramped – and it could be noisy if one or two snored! *Glasgow University Archives*

Left Right at the end of her career, after Sir Alfred Read had ceased to be chairman of Coast Lines, *Ulster Duke* was able to revert to her original Belfast SS Company funnel colours and is seen here in the Mersey on 18 October 1948. *H. B. Christiansen*

October 1966 and was then bought by Greek interests, not finally being scrapped until 1979.

The 1937/8 ships had one major disadvantage – they did not carry cattle. It was decided that their post-war replacements should once again have this facility, without which no self-respecting Irish Sea ship was complete! This in turn meant that they carried rather fewer passengers, but apart from a few peak sailings this was not a drawback. Nor were the buff hulls repeated, the new ships having green hulls with a cream line. With the same names as their predecessors, they both entered service on 5 April 1948 and remained until ousted by the car ferry 20 years later.

The old ships were by no means finished when the new vessels entered service in 1938. Wisely, in view of the deteriorating international situation,

Sir Alfred Read resisted calls for them to be scrapped and they gave yeoman service throughout the war after the more modern vessels had all gone off on active service. *Louth*, formerly *Lady Munster*, had a spell on the LMS Heysham-Belfast service together with *Cambria* from Holyhead, and when the latter was hurriedly recalled to her own service in July 1945, the old ship carried on single-handed. Later she went back to her original service, Liverpool-Belfast, and ended her days as *Ulster Duke*. *Longford* remained as an extra on the Dublin service, latterly carrying many holidaymakers bound for Butlin's holiday camp at Mosney, near Drogheda. She also had some spells on the Belfast service, and it was fitting that it was there that she made her last sailing, on 1 November 1952. She was broken up at Barrow.

Right The Coast Lines empire, as shown on a coloured card of the early 1950s. The large ships in the second row from the front are, from left to right, *Innisfallen*, *Ulster Prince*, *Irish Coast*, *Munster* and *Royal Scotsman*, while in the front row are *Ulster Premier*, *Lairdsloch*, *Caledonian Coast*, *Netherlands Coast* and *Kilkenny*. *Author's collection*

Below The cargo ship *Kilkenny*, built in 1937, sets off down the Liffey in June 1965. *Author*

7. CRUISING

There is no doubt that, almost from the first days of steam vessels, many passengers used them not as a means of getting from A to B, but simply for the pleasure of a sea voyage, which, in the case of the west coast of Scotland, could also be combined with appreciation of marvellous scenery. However, for many years such passengers were viewed as a sideline to the main cargo and passenger business and no special provision was made for them.

The first coasting firm that opened up the cruise market, using Irish Sea ships to sail to the West of Scotland, was Messrs M. Langlands & Sons, whose origins could be traced back to 1836. In 1894 the company acquired *Princess Victoria* (not to be confused with the Stranraer ships of the same name), and seven years later followed her with *Princess Maud*, a ship that could accommodate 140 passengers and whose dining saloon was panelled in carved oak. Advertisements also mentioned that these ships had electric light, spring mattresses in the berths, baths and a piano – all features that were still novelties for such ships at that date. In 1911 the ships were used on 10-day tours to the North of Scotland, for which fares began from £5 5s 0d, inclusive of all meals. No itineraries have come to light, but there must have been opportunities to make excursions to inland destinations, since Loch Maree is mentioned in a list of places visited.

Meanwhile *Princess Alberta* of 1905 gave 'yachting cruises' varying in length from seven to 12 days from Liverpool to the Clyde and such Highland lochs as Loch Duich, Loch Hourn and Loch Swen. Fares started from £4 4s 0d, and to emphasise the yachting aspect the ship had a grey hull instead of the usual black. More adventurous travellers could circumnavigate Britain on *Princess Beatrice* (1891). This trip took 12 days and prices were from £6 15s 0d upwards. Only the last of these survived the First World War, and in 1919 the firm was taken over by Coast Lines Ltd.

Not to be outdone, G. & J. Burns in June 1913 offered a cruise to Iceland via the Western Isles on the company's fairly new *Ermine*; the itinerary is not given, but four days were allowed at Reykjavik. She was built in 1912 for the Dublin service and could take 170 passengers in 1st Class. The exercise was repeated on a few occasions until the First World War intervened. Later links between Scotland and Iceland operated via Leith.

In the 1920s cruises were given again, to western Scottish waters only, the ship used being Burns & Laird Lines' *Tiger*, but she was not ideal, lounge accommodation being limited. In 1923 the charge for a 12-day cruise was £18 18s 0d. A better ship was required and in due course, following the introduction of new motorships by the Coast Lines group in 1929/30, *Killarney*, no longer needed at Cork, was transferred to the parent company in 1931 and completely refurbished to fit her for cruising. She had been built, as *Magic*, for the Belfast SS Company in 1893 and had become successively *Classic* and *Killarney*. With her elegant lines and a new livery of grey hull, white upperworks and buff funnels, she looked every inch a steam yacht and, especially when illuminated at night, made quite an impression at her ports of call. She generally gave seven 13-day and two eight-day cruises form Liverpool, also fitting in a short trip at Whitsun. Fares, which were quoted in guineas, varied according to the type of cabin, but in 1939 that for a berth in a two-berth cabin on the main deck was 17 guineas, which would have been equivalent to about three weeks' salary in a well-paid job. Scottish passengers could join and leave at Ardrossan, for which they had a reduction of 10 shillings. Itineraries varied, but that for what turned out to be her final cruise, leaving Liverpool on 18 August, took her first to the Kyles of Bute, then via Tobermory, Portree and Tarbert (Harris) to Stornoway. She returned via

Right Langland's *Princess Victoria* in the Mersey before 1914. She was built at Dundee by W. B. Thompson & Co and was sunk by the German U-boat U20 off the Mersey Bar on 8 March 1915, the first of many Irish Sea ships to meet that fate. *Courtesy of National Museums Liverpool, Merseyside Maritime Museum*

Below A postcard view of *Princess Maud*, posted in Birkenhead on 23 July 1906, at the end of a cruise. The writer recorded two grand days to finish the cruise, after 30 hours of storms. *Author's collection*

Right An official Langlands' card with a view of Lewes Castle in Stornoway, sent by a passenger on the same ship on 21 August 1903. The building now forms part of Lewes Castle College. *Author's collection*

Stornoway—The Castle.

M. Langlands & Sons' Sea Tours.

S.S. Princess *Maud*

21. VIII. 03

Ermine **on the Clyde; for an unknown reason the name on
her bow has been rather clumsily blacked out.** *Glasgow
University Archives*

Gairloch, Kyle, Fort William and Oban to
Brodick.

While at sea there were ample opportunities for
deck games, and at night whist drives, bridge and
dancing were arranged. Anglers could hire lines to
try sea fishing in northern lochs, and visitors were
warned not to forget their golf clubs, as courses
were open to passengers at many ports of call.

At a date in the 1930s, *Killarney*'s bridge deck
was enclosed to form an observation lounge,
which gave the ship a top-heavy appearance when
viewed from ahead. It was no doubt appreciated by
patrons when a Scottish downpour came on and

the panorama of Scotland's beauty could be
viewed from a comfortable chair, as the brochure
tactfully put it! There was a rather small bar on
board, located in a deckhouse aft on the boat deck,
but for those who preferred to bring their own,
corkage at the rate of 1 shilling per bottle was
charged. The bar closed at 11.00pm and 'lights
out' in the saloons followed at 11.30. Smoking was
not permitted below decks. With these conditions,
and bearing in mind that young children were not
conveyed, the on-board atmosphere must have
been quite peaceful!

For many who sailed in her, idyllic days among
the sea lochs of Scotland must have suggested that
the ship lived up to her original name, but such
days came to an abrupt end when she returned to
Liverpool on Thursday 31 August 1939, to don

An official Belfast SS Company card,
with a sketch of *Magic* in original
condition. James McDowell was
Manager from 1891, when he came
from the Belfast & Northern Counties
Railway, until his death in August
1921. *Author's collection*

Above A view of *Killarney* in the Firth of Clyde. *Author's collection*

COAST LINES LTD.

SCOTTISH FIRTHS & FJORDS CRUISES

S.Y. "KILLARNEY"

Above The first brochures advertising the cruises were adorned with a simple drawing of the ship in an appropriately Scottish setting, but by 1939 the young lady in her slacks struck a note of informality. *Author's collection*

Middle Two lady passengers aboard *Killarney*, clearly enjoying the cruise, are accompanied by a gentleman in a nautical cap. *Author's collection*

Above Passengers, mostly well wrapped up, take a keen interest in a game of shuffleboard. *Author's collection*

Above A game of deck quoits at the after end of *Killarney*'s upper deck. *Author's collection*

Right A younger lady passenger sports very fashionable leisurewear – but why does she look so puzzled? *Author's collection*

Left As it was not always possible for passengers to land at a pier, launches served as tenders at some ports of call. *Author's collection*

naval rather than yachting grey and to face Dunkirk.

For those who could not afford *Killarney*'s prices, or who simply wanted what would now be called a short break, the Belfast SS Company had the answer. Although it was still necessary to have three ships to maintain the Liverpool-Belfast service, one was always spare over the weekend and in 1933 it was decided to use this ship to provide short cruises to Scotland. From 1934 onwards, this was almost always *Ulster Prince*. In 1937 four such cruises were given, leaving Liverpool on Saturdays 15 May, 19 June, 3 July and 14 August. The destinations were either Tobermory and Oban or Arrochar and Oban, and the ship arrived back in Liverpool on Tuesday morning at 7.00am. The fare for a berth in a two-berth cabin was 80 shillings and passengers booking for all four cruises were granted a reduction of 20%. While perhaps somewhat rushed, these cruises were very popular and continued until the outbreak of war.

A rather unusual variant on the theme was tried in the summer of 1938, when *Louth* (the former *Graphic*) was scheduled to make several cruises to Greenock, in connection with the Empire Exhibition being held in Bellahouston Park in Glasgow. For this her funnels were repainted plain yellow. These cruises were to have operated twice weekly, apart from peak weeks in July, but in the event it seems that only three actually ran, on Saturdays 4 June and 30 July and Wednesday 8 June. Possibly the atrocious weather of that summer had killed the demand for a sea trip to the Clyde. The Saturday departures gave a day's cruising on the Clyde and one whole day in Scotland, while the Wednesday sailing gave almost two days to enjoy the Exhibition. Fares were 90 to 120 shillings and 55 to 100 shillings, and passenger numbers were limited.

Above Louth at Greenock on Friday 10 June 1938. *Courtesy of National Museums Liverpool, Merseyside Maritime Museum*

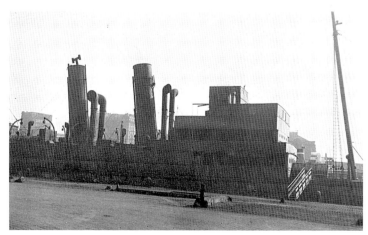

Right Killarney in a rather sorry condition in 1946. *Author's collection*

Lady Killarney, **with buff hull, off Liverpool landing stage on 2 June 1949.** *H. B. Christiansen*

When peace returned, *Killarney* (later renamed *Lady Killarney*) seemed to be beyond repair – although as will be seen, she still had plenty of life left in her – and in her place the former *Patriotic/Lady Connaught* was reconditioned for the role of cruising yacht. It helped that she now had considerable refrigeration capacity from her days as a hospital ship. She was given a new restaurant, a new entrance saloon, a card room on her lower deck and a bar in a deckhouse on the boat deck. Given that austerity still prevailed, it appears that the work was carried out to a very high standard. Unfortunately Coast Lines' predilection for 'Olde English' once again got the better of it and the new smoke room was in the style of an ancient village pub. Otherwise the refurbished ship brought a most welcome splash of colour to the Mersey when she re-appeared in March 1947 in her new livery of buff hull and funnel, with white upperworks and green boot topping – in fact, she could have been mistaken for a miniature Orient liner. This brave colour scheme proved to be impracticable and, after a brief period with a green hull, she was painted in Coast Lines' more sombre but still dignified black and white livery from 1952. She was withdrawn at the end of the 1956 season and broken up at Port Glasgow.

As with *Killarney,* she performed eight 13-day

cruises, but there were rather more shorter trips available; in 1949 there were three six-day cruises, and four in 1951. Fares had of course risen, and in 1951 that for a berth in a two-berth cabin for 13 days was between 38 and 45 guineas, making her, in relation to the cost of living, more expensive than her predecessor had been. The same deck games were provided, but a novelty in 1952 was a cricket match in Skye between a team from the ship and a local team gathered from the island and mainland Ross-shire; the winning side is not recorded. There were plans to use *Irish Coast* on cruising from 1957 onwards, but the urgent need to replace *Lairds Isle* meant that she was required elsewhere and Coast Lines withdrew from the business. She would have probably been very successful in such work.

However, this was not quite the end of cruising by Irish Sea ships. In 1958 British Railways decided to fill the gap left by Coast Lines and placed its almost-new *Duke of Lancaster* on a series of cruises to Scottish waters and also to European cities. These were run in May, June and September, when the ship was not required for relief work at Heysham. Usually the first was for six days, and those in June and September were for ten days. The ship visited the more frequented parts of the West Highlands, Portree, Stornoway and Tobermory, and there were no side trips into remote lochs. This practice lasted until 1966, in which year she made four Scottish trips, as well as

Above The brochure for cruises by *Duke of Lancaster* in 1966. *Author's collection*

Above right Passengers enjoying a meal in the dining saloon. *Lancaster City Museums*

Below *Duke of Lancaster* at Inveraray on 24 May 1960. As can be seen, it was usual to dress her overall when calling at a port. As it was not possible for her to come alongside the pier, either here or at any other port of call except Stornoway, one of the ship's lifeboats was used as a tender. *Ian S. Pearsall, courtesy of Alan W. H. Pearsall*

one each to Scandinavia and to Spain and Portugal. A double-berth outside cabin on B Deck cost £50 per person for the longer Scottish cruise in 1966, perhaps rather better value than with Coast Lines. These cruises were certainly popular and there was regret from patrons who had returned year after year when they were discontinued; the ship was now required full-time at Heysham, as her sister *Duke of Rothesay*, converted to a side-loading car ferry, had been transferred to Fishguard, and the Scottish lochs cruise that ended at Heysham on 24 September 1966 was to be her last.

As *Duke of Lancaster* was not a full-time cruise ship, a good deal of work had been needed to make her suitable for the role. Some cabins were transformed into bathrooms for adjacent cabins, one was fitted out as a hairdressing salon, one

The cover of the Clyde Shipping Company programme for 1937. *Dr A. C. Harper collection*

lounge became a ballroom, and the 2nd Class cafeteria became a restaurant. Numbers were limited to 350. It was hard work for the crew, who were recruited from all the Heysham ships on a voluntary basis, but there was never any shortage of manpower.

Additionally, apart from designated cruises there were until 1939 plenty of opportunities to enjoy the Irish Sea and visit Irish ports in ships that were basically employed on cargo services. The main company to provide such sailings was the Clyde Shipping Company, an old-established concern whose services had at one time been used by many cross-channel passengers. After 1918 few used them as a means of travelling from place to place, but many used them as cruises, and the Company actively encouraged this development. The last two ships built before 1939, *Rathlin* and *Beachy*, were fitted with attractive observation lounges under the bridge to increase their appeal, and some older ships were also given this feature. The standard of catering on board seems to have been one of the main reasons why this operator built up a large clientele of regulars.

In 1937 holidaymakers starting from Glasgow could choose from four weekly departures. On Mondays there was a sailing to Belfast, Waterford, Plymouth and London, arriving there on the following Sunday. Tuesdays saw two departures, to Belfast, Southampton and London, and to Dublin, Waterford and Cork. On Fridays there was a direct sailing to London via Belfast. There was also a single sailing from Ardrossan to London, arriving there on Friday morning. The cabin fare from Glasgow to London was 55 shillings single and £5 return, and steerage single fares were also offered, at 25 shillings; these did not include meals. However, cruising passengers were probably more interested in round trips, such as Glasgow to Plymouth and back – 1,200 miles for 80 shillings. Passengers were allowed to sleep on board at Plymouth and thus save on hotel expenses.

There were also attractive trips available in conjunction with the companies operating on the East Coast, the Dundee, Perth & London Shipping Company and the London & Edinburgh Shipping Company. A cruise to London and back from either Leith or Dundee could be had for 85 shillings in cabin only, and excursions were available at the various ports of call. Passengers in

Right A Clyde Shipping Company postcard. *Author's collection*

Below *Beachy* as built, on a CSC postcard. She was sunk in 1940 while serving as a rescue ship. *Author's collection*

Right *Copeland* at an unknown location in the 1930s, after she had been given an observation lounge below the bridge. *Author's collection*

A lady passenger, probably Miss McQueen, on board *Fastnet*. At this time the ship was normally employed on the Glasgow-Cork service, which allowed passengers almost a whole day in Dublin and a morning in Waterford. *Andrew McQueen collection, Glasgow University Archives*

Belfast could take a tram to see the new parliament buildings at Stormont, or go to Bellevue Park. At Waterford a jaunting-car trip made a bit of variety, though the charge of 14 shillings for the return trip of 14 miles to Tramore would seem to be on the expensive side, and that resort could just as easily be reached by train from Waterford Manor station, near where the ship berthed. From Plymouth the Western National Omnibus Company offered a bargain of 75 miles across Dartmoor to Torquay for only 7 shillings. What was called the 'victualling department' provided breakfast at 8.30am, dinner at 1 o'clock and tea at 6.30pm, the charges being 3, 4 and 3 shillings respectively. Plain breakfasts and teas were also available at lower prices, and supper was served, time unspecified, for 2 shillings. Relaxing in the bar of an evening, one could enjoy a whisky for 1s 8d or a bottle of beer at 9d. Claret was on the wine list, but there is no mention of white wine. The bar closed at 11.00pm.

It has to be said that the on-board accommodation was not spacious. The ships used on these cruise sailings all had a small smoke room or lounge on the upper deck, a dining saloon below this and a row of cabins along each side of the promenade deck. Even on the newest ships, *Rathlin* and *Beachy*, seating in the saloon was at long tables for eight diners. At the height of the season extra berths were made up in the smoke room, for which an allowance was made against the fare, this being 5 shillings in the case of the Glasgow to London route. However, no matter how tired they might have been, passengers occupying those berths could not go to bed until after the smoke room closed at 11.00pm!

Those who wanted to complete a circumnavigation of Britain could use the ships of the Antrim Iron Ore Company, which, rather improbably, catered for cargo passengers in a manner similar to the Clyde Shipping Company. The company's ships, *Glentaise* and *Glendun* (in 1928) ran from Belfast to Stockton via the North of Scotland, and round-trip passengers had the pleasure of three whole days in the latter port; presumably they went on tours to inland sights in Durham and Yorkshire. Calls were made at Leith, and a Belfast-Edinburgh return was available for £3 17s 0d. The passenger and cargo service was taken over by Coast Lines in August 1929.

All these and other coastal cruises came to an end in 1939 and were not resumed after the war. Only Coast Lines kept the tradition alive into the 1960s with *Caledonian Coast* and *Hibernian Coast*, which ran 10-day round trips between Liverpool and London, calling for two days at Dublin on the return voyage. These ships were built by Hall, Russell & Company at Aberdeen in 1948 and 1947 respectively. Eleven passengers were carried in single and two-berth cabins and there was a pleasant lounge and dining saloon. In 1965 the round-trip fare in a single cabin was £57 10s 0d. These trips came to an end in the late 1960s.

Right A brochure advertising the trips. *Author's collection*

Below The motorship *Pacific Coast*, built by the Ardrossan Dockyard in 1947, was also used on the Coast Lines cruises. *Author's collection*

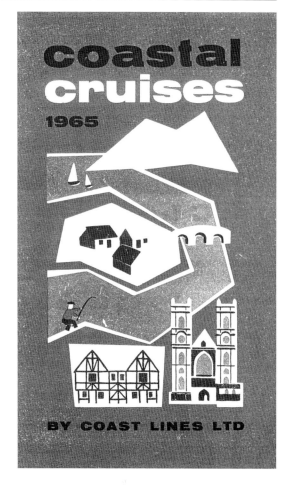

8. THE REVOLUTIONARY *ULSTER MONARCH*

In 1928 Sir Alfred Read, Chairman of the Belfast Steam Ship Company, obtained approval from the board to order two revolutionary new cross-channel ships for the Liverpool-Belfast overnight service. The order went to Harland & Wolff, and a third ship was later added to this. The propulsion machinery marked a complete break with tradition, since it consisted of two ten-cylinder, four-stroke diesel engines, manufactured by the builders. The credit for this innovation was divided equally between Sir Alfred and Charles Payne, Managing Director of Harland & Wolff. The cost of each ship was in the region of £260,000. The coal-burning turbine

An official card of the ship when new. *Author's collection*

'Dukes', which the LMS had just acquired for its Heysham-Belfast route, cost only £216,000 each, but it was estimated that the BSSC would now save about £20,000 per annum in fuel costs with the new ships.

Ulster Monarch, the first and ultimately the most famous of the trio, entered service on 11 June 1929. For those in 1st Class, there was a spacious dining saloon at the after end of B deck, separated from the entrance vestibule, with its purser's office and shop, by an attractive wood and glass screen. The lounge was above it on A deck, and on the upper deck were the smoke room and verandah café. The cabin accommodation was forward of the public rooms and in all offered 411 berths in single- and two-berth cabins, almost all of which

The smoke room used oak panelling, mullion windows and antique wall lights to create the impression of an Tudor English village inn. *Author's collection*

had a porthole. Probably the innovation most welcomed by the travelling public was the provision of hot water in all cabins. There were also four two-berth cabins-de-luxe on A deck, these being en suite. Aft, 3rd Class passengers had 80 berths and a large cafeteria. In a striking livery of grey hull, white upperworks and the usual BSSC red funnel with black top, the new ships caught the eye wherever they went and were an excellent advertisement for the company. It had apparently decided that it had inherited the role of catering for the Anglo-Irish ascendancy from the City of Dublin Company and now styled itself Ulster Imperial Line. However, the name did not catch on with the public and was dropped after 1945.

Innovatory the ships may have been in the technical field, but they were anything but that when it came to the design of the passenger accommodation. Although it was all most comfortable, the public rooms harked back to the time when ships' saloons tried to re-create the atmosphere of a great house on shore, perhaps in an attempt to persuade passengers that they actually were on shore! The accompanying illustrations show how this was done.

Ulster Monarch had a long and very successful career, not being withdrawn until 2 October 1966. She also had a distinguished war record, including a circumnavigation of Africa and taking part in D-Day. She almost met her end on 18 August 1943 when she was attacked by an aircraft off Cape Bon

and caught fire. However, she made it back to Tripoli, where repairs took a fortnight, and took part in the first landing of troops on the Italian mainland in the following month. Rightly the company took great pride in her achievements and a little book was published about them after the war.

This theme was carried through into the verandah café, which, with its opening on to the boat deck, made an attractive rendezvous, especially when the ships were used for cruising. *Author's collection*

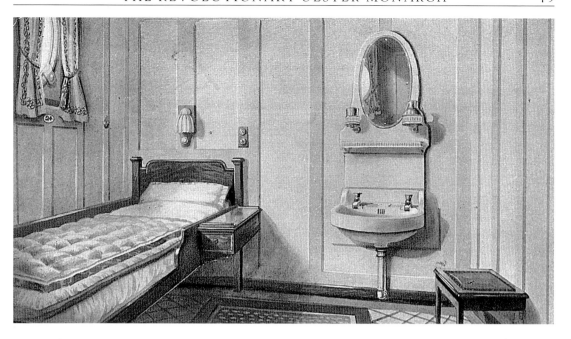

Top left The lounge, with polished grey wood and red-and-white-striped chairs, had a distinct touch of Regency about it. *Author's collection*

Middle left The restaurant was furnished in Louis XVI style. It was panelled in mahogany and the curtains and the shaded table lamps were pink. *Author's collection*

Bottom left One of the cabins-de-luxe. *Author's collection*

Top A single-berth cabin in 1st Class. *Author's collection*

Middle and bottom It is unfair to be too critical. Passengers loved the new ships, and a comparison with the rather gloomy single-berth cabin and the restaurant with its fixed swivel chairs seen here on one of the previous generation of ships shows just how great the improvement was. These are the restaurant on a ship of the 'Graphic' Class, and a single-berth cabin on *Patriotic* of 1912. *Author's collection*

Above As altered after war service and with a black hull, *Ulster Monarch* lies at Donegall Quay on 3 August 1964. *Author*

Below Her running mate, *Ulster Prince*, at the same berth a few days earlier. *Author*

9. RUNNING A LARGE MARINE DEPARTMENT: THE LNWR 1883-98

North Wall

The involvement of the London & North Western Railway in Ireland had begun as far back as 1861, when it joined with the Midland & Great Western – the railway that handled the greatest livestock trade in Ireland – and the Duke of Leinster to set up a company to build a new cattle market at the North Wall, on the River Liffey. Unfortunately the bill to permit this was not successful and the new market was constructed two years later in Prussia Street. Forty years on,

A view of the exterior of North Wall station in May 1886.
National Railway Museum

James Joyce was moved to complain about the noise and smell caused by the animals being driven through the streets from the market down to the North Wall. But the M&GWR did construct its Liffey branch to a point near the North Wall, and relations between the English and Irish companies remained cordial.

In 1872 the LNWR also became closely involved with the Great Southern & Western Railway, to the extent of contributing £90,000 towards the construction of a link from Islandbridge Junction to meet the M&GWR line and other works to bring G&SWR trains to North Wall. The Great Northern also built a connection. The LNWR built a line to Newcomen Bridge

Junction and also a station and capacious siding accommodation at North Wall. Even as late as 1965 a large sign on the roof of a shed proudly proclaimed 'British Railways Dublin North Wall'.

The station opened in November 1877 and was connected to the quayside by two tunnels for passengers. In 1878 the adjacent Prince of Wales Hotel was acquired and extended by new buildings to the rear. Later the original building was replaced by a new one, this work being finished in 1890, and attractive gardens were laid out, a distinct amenity in this part of the city. The hotel also provided breakfast baskets to those landing from the night steamer and going on by connecting trains. As there was a shortage of decent housing in the area, the LNWR also built some new houses in New Wapping Street and bought others in the area. Through carriages were worked to Broadstone and Kingsbridge stations and in October 1896 the LNWR secured the contract to carry letters which had arrived too late in Liverpool to catch Cunard liners. This required a through train form North Wall to Queenstown, which continued until 1914. The conclusion of James Joyce's short story 'Eveline' gives a good idea of how the station would have seemed to a boat passenger about 1904.

While passengers appreciated the convenience of the terminal at North Wall, navigation on the Liffey posed problems for LNWR masters throughout the period when it was in use. Quite simply, the river was too congested with ships of all kinds, some of which did not obey the basic rules, such as displaying lights at night, and it seemed that the Dublin Port & Docks Board, while happy enough to collect dues, was slow to take any measures to improve matters. Some accidents were trivial, such as that on 15 November 1890 when *Shamrock* fouled the bowsprit of the trawler *Citizen*, whose owners received £5 in compensation to avoid litigation. Others verged on the comical, as that on 8 January 1883 when *Rose* collided with a dredger that had been left in the middle of the channel without lights. A few led to fatalities: on 2 May 1889 the engines of the cargo steamer *Irene* were turned over prior to her departure and a small boat, which was under her stern, was sunk and a boy drowned. Admiral Dent was told to deal with the ship's engineer, but it is not recorded that any payment was made to the parents of the lad.

As there was insufficient room at North Wall, ships had to be berthed with bow or stern overlapping, and on occasions they also overlapped Dublin & Glasgow S&SP Company's ships, leading to damage. After £5 7s 8d had been paid to the latter company in April 1893, orders were given that this practice should cease. There were also collisions with other cross-channel ships. When taking action to avoid a barge in February 1886, *Shamrock* damaged the Glasgow steamer *Duke of Leinster* to a value of £10. *Irene* was in trouble again on 16 October 1894 when she damaged the City of Dublin Company's *Longford* while swinging at North Wall, and £7

Shamrock (on the left) and the rather older *Duchess of Sutherland* at North Wall. On the extreme right is the original hotel, with work going ahead on the extension to the rear, suggesting that the photograph dates from about 1879. To the left of the hotel, the covered footbridge that linked it to the station can be seen. *London & North Western Railway Society*

had to be paid to avoid litigation. It could have been worse.

Having effectively created a British railway enclave, the LNWR sought a manager who would be competent to run such a varied enterprise, involving railwaymen, dock workers, hotel staff and clerical workers, and the man appointed was a Mr J. Roberts, who did not last long in the post. He was succeeded in 1869 by Mr W. G. Skipworth, who did a great deal to make a success of the business. He died in 1898 and was succeeded by Henry G. Burgess, a native of Tipperary. He was an extremely capable manager and was very successful at North Wall, although he did have a tendency to take for or against particular individuals, and one of those he took against was James Larkin, with whom he once had a memorable row by telephone. However, he could also be tactful. In 1917 the British government requisitioned four cargo ships of the City of Dublin company and proposed to put these under the management of the LNWR, Whitehall having no idea of the history of inter-company relations on the Irish Sea. Burgess immediately pointed out that the LNWR did not have statutory powers to operate to the Mersey and the ships were finally handed over to the British & Irish Steam Packet Company for the duration of the war.

Henry Burgess certainly needed all his skill in industrial relations in the years during and after the First World War, in which his own son was killed. After the proclamation of the republic at Easter 1916 and the associated repression, almost 500 of those involved were shipped from North Wall to Holyhead in one of the cargo steamers. They were imprisoned in the hold with no toilet facilities, and it was a rough crossing. When the ship arrived at Holyhead, the atmosphere was foul, reminiscent of the 'coffin ships' of the late 1840s.

In 1918 there was a one-day strike against the introduction of conscription in Ireland. As General French's campaign of repression continued, the War of Independence began and one of the first victims was the Irish trade unionist William O'Brien, who was imprisoned in England, where he went on hunger strike. In London Mr Burgess met the Home Secretary to plead, unsuccessfully, on his behalf – although he was later released.

It was at North Wall on 20 May 1920 that the port workers refused to handle munitions destined for the British forces, leading to a widespread and prolonged lock-out and strike, which did not end until 14 December. However, no worker who had taken part in the dispute was victimised. On top of all this, there were 'normal' industrial difficulties connected with the transfer of some staff to what had just become Dun Laoghaire, following the granting of the mail contract to the LNWR.

Matters became even worse in 1921 when the Auxiliaries took over the now-closed hotel and made it their headquarters. On 11 April there was a pitched battle around the hotel, in which a number of staff took part, though fortunately none of these was killed. It was a tribute to all the efforts he had made towards a negotiated peace settlement and all the times that he had spoken out against extremism on both sides that Mr Burgess was made both a British Privy Councillor by Lloyd George in 1921 and in 1924 also a member of the Irish Free State senate by W. T. Cosgrave. In 1924 he became General Manager of the new LMS, but continued to maintain a close interest in cross-channel matters; he also became the LMS board member of the new Great Southern Railways.

In due course peace came, but the great days of North Wall were over. Already, in 1908, following an attempt by the Dublin Port Board to increase dues on LNWR ships, the day express had been transferred to Kingstown, much to the annoyance of the City of Dublin Company, which not only mounted a legal challenge but sought to keep out LNWR ships by the expedient of blocking the arrival berth at Carlisle Pier by one of its own ships. Sinn Fein then got in on the act by claiming that Irish jobs were at risk. This was not the case, as the LNWR simply transferred the staff it needed, but it made good political capital. However, it may well have been difficult for some of those who lived in the North Wall area to commute daily, as the Dublin tramways did not offer workmen's fares and the journey would have taken an hour in each direction. The City Company lost the legal battle in the High Court and the latter practice was ultimately ended only through the tact of the harbour master at Kingstown and his assistant. When the LNWR secured the mail contract, the night service also went to Kingstown and the only passenger traffic remaining at North Wall was that of the drovers and cattle dealers who used the cargo boats. The passenger station closed in 1923, but the livestock trade remained as busy as ever until the economic wars of the 1930s began.

Holyhead

The centre of the LNWR's marine activities was Holyhead. Not only was its own fleet controlled from and repaired there, but there was a considerable measure of influence over the design of the ships for the two other routes in which the company had an interest, namely the Fleetwood-Belfast and Stranraer-Larne services. The Marine Superintendent of the LNWR was the final arbiter in any matters of debate.

In the 1860s ships had to be reboilered quite frequently and the company became annoyed at the excessive charges made and the length of time taken by outside firms to do this work. In 1863 the Board agreed to a proposal that there should be at Holyhead a well-equipped workshop that could carry out this work, and the first new boilers were fitted to *Admiral Moorsom* in 1868. By 1883 the facilities had grown into quite a large industrial complex, known as the Marine Yard and employing 150 men in the 1890s. The yard was located at the north end of the western quay, with a good view over the inner harbour towards the station. The office and stores building faced the water and also had a meetings room, all on the first floor. Behind it were the fitting shop, erecting shop and boiler shop. There was also a smithy and a sawmill and separate workshops for sailmakers, carpenters, upholsterers and polishers. From 1900, when the station and surrounding buildings were fitted with electric light, there was also a department for electricians. The buildings still stand and it is good to record that the offices were renovated in a sympathetic manner by Stena Line in 2004 and are now used by the technical and marine departments of that company.

Rather unusually, the LNWR did not have a separate committee to oversee its shipping services until the last year of its independent existence. These were instead governed mainly by the locomotive committee, though both the passenger and goods committees also had a say and the Board itself took a close interest in matters marine. The creation of special committees of the Board, which usually met in the Chairman's room, was a fairly regular occurrence, as and when any particularly difficult question arose. Ships' names were also frequently decided by one of these special committees, and this probably explains the choice of the names *Eleanor* (Sir Richard Moon's daughter) and *Edith* (his wife).

This may sound like a recipe for confusion and inter-departmental rivalry, but in practice the system seems to have worked quite smoothly, possibly because of the strong personality of Admiral C. B. C. Dent, who was Marine Superintendent from 1865 until 28 February 1893. He had come from the Royal Navy and when he was finally persuaded to retire – there seems to have been some friction with the Board about this – he was replaced by Captain William H. Binney from the Pacific Steam Navigation Company, an equally determined officer! These two men set the tone for the entire service and ensured its success in a difficult and highly competitive field. Captain Binney's salary was £700 per annum, together with a house at Holyhead, which was put in order at the Company's expense before he moved in. He must have made a good impression, since his salary was increased to £800 from 1 January 1895 on the recommendation of the Chairman.

The departure of Admiral Dent led to a visit to Holyhead by four directors, the General Manager and Mr Webb on 20 June 1893. Perhaps this was their first chance for some time to see for themselves how matters stood, but if they expected to find much amiss they were clearly disappointed, and their report was something of a damp squib. The main two recommendations were that the tickets of passengers should be inspected when they embarked, and that the hotel laundry in London Road should be enlarged to allow it to deal with the ships' linen; this latter recommendation would allow the company to take over this function from the individual captains, who had previously contracted the work out to the washerwomen of Holyhead. At the same time, the company took over from the captains the running of on-board catering, and this was also managed through the hotel, although a separate catering department was set up in 1905.

While the managers did not have to live with the threat of consultants breathing down their necks, there were occasions when they had to take time off from running a fleet to deal with other matters; in July 1895 Captain Binney was told to submit plans for moving the men's latrines from under the general office at Holyhead where they were a) offensive and b) could not be supervised. It is not clear what had been going on, nor how the Captain resolved the matter!

The main competitor was, of course, the City of Dublin Steam Packet Company, whose ships also sailed from Holyhead to what was then Kingstown and which had, from 1860 until 1920, the mail contract. The new facilities at Holyhead had of course been constructed to improve the railway's chances of gaining the contract when it came up for renewal, and success seemed to have crowned its efforts when, in January 1883, the LNWR was awarded the contract. There had also been a good deal of lobbying in London. Mr John Laird of the Birkenhead shipyard was then asked to meet a committee made up of Sir Richard Moon, Mr Plunkett, Mr T. H. Ismay (of the White Star Line) and Admiral Dent to discuss designs for improved steamers with compound engines. However, the award of the contract to the LNWR provoked a furious row between Gladstone's Liberal government and the Irish MPs (of all political views) at Westminster. Given that he was attempting to pacify Ireland and would very soon bring in his first Home Rule bill, this was something that Gladstone could not afford, and in due course the LNWR was asked by the Postmaster-General to withdraw its tender and a new contract was awarded to the Dublin company. The LNWR Board was furious, but there was little they could do about the matter and had to look for other methods to maintain their relative position on the London-Dublin axis. The LNWR was also unsuccessful in 1895 – though this time there was less acrimony –

and it was not until 1920 that it finally gained the coveted contract. But it was a pyrrhic victory. The general election of 1918 and the creation of Dail Eireann had already ended the commuting of Irish MPs between Dublin and London. Just 13 months later the agreement that gave Ireland her independence was signed, and from March 1922 all the official traffic vanished, and with it the kudos of the former mail service. Of course there was still plenty of commercial and personal mail, and there was still some official mail for the six counties that remained part of the United Kingdom, but even that was diverted to Stranraer in 1923. The glory days were definitely over!

Realising at quite an early date that it would have to compete with the City of Dublin company by offering a superior service, the LNWR began by improving its facilities at Holyhead, where its ships used the inner harbour. Although this was

*This view looking inwards from the entrance to the harbour was taken between 1880 and 1884. The single-funnelled ship is **Admiral Moorsom**, the first vessel to be built for the LNWR. Captain, later Admiral, C. R. Moorsom was a director of the Chester & Holyhead Railway, and acted as unofficial marine superintendent until Captain T. Hirste was appointed in that capacity in 1850. This ship was constructed in 1860 by Randolph, Elder & Co of Glasgow (predecessors of the Fairfield Company) and inaugurated the service to North Wall on 1 October of that year. She was reboilered in 1866, losing one funnel in the process. On 15 January 1885 she was lost by collision with a US steamer. Ahead of her lies either **Lily** or **Violet**, and a dredger, sent round from Garston, is busy in the harbour. The obelisk on the hill behind commemorates Commander J. MacG. Skinner, who, as captain of the Post Office steam packet **Lightning** carried King George IV to Ireland in August 1821. Sadly Skinner was drowned at sea on 13 October 1832 when a huge wave swept him overboard from the packet **Escape**, within sight of Holyhead. London & North Western Railway Society*

Above Another view of the harbour, probably taken on the day of its formal opening, 1 July 1880. On the left is the brand new *Lily*, which has just returned from a short cruise with distinguished guests, including the Prince of Wales. On the right is the Greenore steamer *Earl Spencer*. *London & North Western Railway Society*

Below Although entitled 'The Irish Mail at Holyhead', it is much more likely that the train in this 1908 view of the new station facilities is connecting with the LNWR's own sailing. *National Railway Museum*

government-owned, it seems that the railway company had a fairly free hand and used this opportunity to lay out one of the best-designed train-ship interchanges in Britain. Separate berths were provided for incoming and outgoing ships, each having its own covered platform, and the transfer from ship to train and vice versa could be made without any exposure to the elements.

It was all a complete contrast to what was known as the Admiralty Pier, from which the mail steamers sailed. This was out on the breakwater and, apart from a commemorative arch recording King George IV's departure for Ireland in 1821, had nothing to commend it to the passenger. As the pier could not take the weight of main-line locomotives, the 'Irish Mail', having dashed down from Euston at high speed, had to be coupled to a small tank engine to trundle down the pier, and there was much less cover for passengers boarding or disembarking. A five-storey hotel was also built at the station and the new facilities were opened for traffic in 1880.

At the Admiralty Pier the ships turned round, or 'swung', ready for the next trip to Kingstown. If all ships were running according to schedule there was no problem, but if the LNWR ships were late in arriving or departing, they could arrive at the pier just as the City of Dublin's mailboat was swinging, and were then further delayed. Thus on 6 April 1887 *Banshee* was detained for 50 minutes by the mailboat, and when she finally reached the inner harbour, she could not come alongside the arrivals berth and had to land her passengers at the departure berth, from which they had the inconvenience of walking a couple of hundred yards to the waiting train. Much the same happened to *Lily* on 20 September of the same

Above About 20 years later, some well-dressed passengers climb the gangway from the 'Irish Mail' on to the steamer. Railway staff attend to the pile of luggage in the background – people did not then travel light! *National Railway Museum*

Right A feature of Holyhead was the provision of a graving dock, which allowed the LNWR, and later the LMS and British Railways, to undertake all routine maintenance of the ships 'in house'. It was rather inconveniently located on the other side of the harbour from the office and workshops, on what was known as the 'Turkey shore', and workmen travelled to and from it on what must have been the smallest craft in the LNWR fleet, a little boat that could take 20 passengers and also materials. It was known as 'Handy Billy' and lasted a good deal longer than some of its more famous cousins, but was ultimately replaced by road transport in the form of a Scammell 'mechanical horse'. The ships dealt with included some from other routes, and here the Stranraer *Princess Margaret* is under repair. *London & North Western Railway Society*

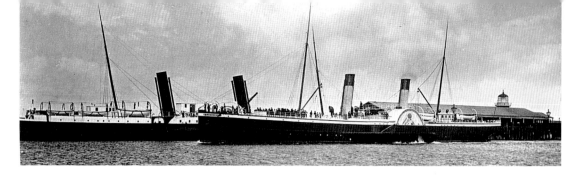

Above Inbound to Holyhead, *Rose* of the LNWR passes one of the City of Dublin Company's paddle steamers at the Admiralty Pier. The latter has already turned around, or swung, to allow her to make a quick start on her next voyage to Kingstown. This practice led to a good deal of friction between the two operators. *Rose* and her sister *Shamrock* inaugurated the day express service when they appeared in 1876. *McLean Museum & Art Gallery, Inverclyde Council*

Below A fine study of *Violet* leaving Holyhead. Together with her sister *Lily* she was built by Laird Bros at Birkenhead in 1880 for the new express night service. Curiously, given F. W. Webb's later interest in compound locomotives, and that compound marine engines were no longer a novelty, these ships, and the later *Banshee* of 1883, were fitted with simple oscillating engines, which provided a smooth motion at the expense of the consumption of a great deal of coal. Much of what went into the furnaces subsequently came out of the funnels, to descend on the decks in the form of unburnt particles. When *Banshee* was later fitted with retarders, it was reported with satisfaction that the latter problem had greatly diminished and that the 'flaming from the funnels had ceased'. The vision of a large steamer, especially one with such a name, proceeding towards Ireland with flames spouting from her funnels must have been upsetting to passengers of a nervous disposition. No doubt the lower capital cost of simple engines had something to do with the decision, but the LNWR had by 1886 begun to regret its penny-pinching attitude. At a meeting in the Chairman's room on 17 November of that year, it was decided that the two ships should be considered for compounding when they required new boilers. Subsequently Messrs Laird offered to fit new compound engines at a cost of £25,000 per ship, but at another meeting in the Chairman's room on 17 November 1887 it was decided not to proceed with this, in view of the age of the ships. They were reboilered in 1888, but the basic problem remained and on 17 May 1889 the Board considered a letter from Laird's, outlining the various possibilities. Fitting compound engines would cost £26,000 per ship, while triple-expansion engines would cost either £29,000 or £36,000, for horsepower of 3,500 or 4,000 respectively. It was decided to adopt the last of these, together with new boilers, with forced draught, at a cost of £10,000 per ship. *Violet* accordingly went back to her builders on 11 April 1890, to be fitted with triple-expansion engines and new locomotive-type boilers of higher pressure. While there her saloon was re-upholstered by Miller & Beatty of Dublin, which had put in the lowest tender of £182 7s 6d, and electric light was installed in the cabins. The work was not completed until 16 December and, when *Violet* went on trial, an exhaust pipe broke. There were sensational reports in the press and this led to a letter from the Board of Trade. After a new pipe had been fitted, trials were run on 2 January 1891, when she performed very well. Her sister followed in 1891. The results were most satisfactory – the ships were now 1 knot faster and a great deal more economical, although Mr Webb had some problems with the dynamos, which tended to run hot. New steel paddle wheels were fitted by the builders in 1895, when the settees in the dining saloons were replaced by individual chairs; in this form they lasted until 1898. By then the boilers were again due for renewal, and on 12 August the Board decided to order two new twin-screw ships to take their place. Apart from the saga of their engines, both ships seem to have led uneventful lives, the worst incident being on 14 March 1887 when the after port boiler on *Violet* was burned. As a result her chief engineer was given notice with six months pay, the second and third engineers were dismissed without pay, and the chief stoker was demoted. *Lily* was withdrawn in 1900 and her sister in 1902, both passing into the ownership of Liverpool & Douglas Steamers Ltd, which was vainly attempting to compete with the Isle of Man SP Company. When this failed, both were scrapped. *McLean Museum & Art Gallery, Inverclyde Council*

year. The LNWR grumbled and ultimately compiled a list of such detentions, but could not really do anything about the matter, given the priority accorded to the mail service. In November 1895 a telephone line, for which the City Company paid half the cost, was put in between the station and the mailboat berth, so that each operator could know what the other was doing, but the problem continued until the CDSPC disappeared for Holyhead.

The depth of water in the inner harbour remained a problem and there were numerous cases of vessels grounding, *Rose* being particularly liable to do so; on 20 March 1893 she was stuck fast for 85 minutes. Apart from a tug/tender named *Cambria*, which was at Holyhead from 1889 to 1896, the LNWR did not station any auxiliary vessels there for many years, but dredgers and hoppers were sometimes sent round from Garston to work on the harbour after spring tides. In 1894 this exercise required the services of two dredgers and two hoppers and cost £2,600. Finally, in 1902 a hopper/dredger named *Pick Me Up* was bought from Fleming & Ferguson of Paisley and permanently stationed at Holyhead, where she worked on the inner harbour eight hours per day, five days a week. She served Holyhead until 1968, when she went off, under her own steam, to be scrapped in Germany; her machinery is preserved in Paisley.

As all ships were, until the arrival of *Princess Maud*, coal-burners, the LNWR acquired two coal hoppers, named *Nancy* and *Herald*, which, by means of conveyor belts and a chute, could load 200 tons of coal per hour into a ship. This operation took place on the side of the ship away from the quay and jets of water were played on to the coal to minimise dust. Enough coal was usually spilled into the harbour to provide fuel for *Pick Me Up*, which simply followed a coal hopper when she required a top-up! The LNWR also maintained a store of coal at Holyhead, and in April 1894 this was increased to 4,500 tons, after industrial relations problems in the coal industry.

The next area to be addressed was on-board amenities. While it would have been difficult to surpass those in 1st Class on the mail steamers, the steerage on the latter was cramped in layout and devoid of even the most basic comforts. Beginning with *Rosstrevor* on the Greenore route and continuing with *Cambria* of 1897 on the express service, the company provided adequate covered accommodation in 3rd Class for all those travelling at off-peak times. In one sense, those in 3rd Class had an advantage over those in the superior class: no general lounge was provided in the latter and any group of friends wishing to get together on board could only do so in one of the private cabins, whereas those in 3rd Class could socialise in the communal accommodation.

Consideration of the needs of the poorer travellers actually began with the rail journey, since the LNWR admitted passengers travelling 3rd Class to the trains connecting with its sailings from an early date, whereas these were barred from the 'Irish Mail' trains until 1 January 1897. Just before that, in 1892, the Traffic Department also began to issue tickets for 3rd Class rail and 1st steamer. No doubt these were aimed at the growing number of middle-class passengers, who could not afford 1st Class throughout the journey, but could pay the difference for added comfort on the sea passage. This development greatly annoyed Admiral Dent, who complained that 'at the most sensitive part of their passage, they [the 1st Class passengers] are incommoded and crowded out … these passengers do not bluster and threaten but quietly take themselves away and we do not see them again.' His solution was to incorporate an additional saloon for 1st Class passengers only, trying it on *Banshee* if she was rebuilt. However, nothing was done about this, and worse was to come shortly afterwards, when the Passenger Committee decided to allow live eels and dogs to be conveyed on the express boats. Again the Admiral objected, saying that this affected his position in the Company, but to no effect. But some class distinctions persisted: in 1st Class passengers were either 'ladies' or 'gentlemen', but in steerage they were simply female or male.

It should not be imagined that those in 1st Class always travelled in the lap of luxury. Until the late 1880s the mattresses in the cabins were simply pallets laid on a wooden board. In 1893 spring mattresses were ordered for the two night boats, at a cost of £39 13s 8d per ship. In 1897 the Passenger Committee noted that the ladies' cabins on board the express steamers accommodated only 38 on sofa berths, and at busy times extra berths had to be made up on the floor. How ladies attired in full

Victorian finery actually coped with sleeping on the floor is not recorded. However, it was found possible to fit 26 additional 'portable' berths, made by Hoskins & Sons of Birmingham, at a cost of £52 10s 8d per vessel. Just two years previously the Board had decided that blankets should be issued for use in ladies' cabins.

Another way in which the LNWR showed its concern for passengers' welfare was by not sailing in very bad weather. The mail ships sailed whatever conditions obtained on the Irish Sea and were driven flat out, to ensure that the timetable laid down in the contract was kept – penalties for delay were severe. The ships, especially those of 1897, were long, and narrow in proportion to their length, designed to be driven head-first into the seas at high speed, and they were therefore notorious rollers. The LNWR did not attempt to match the speeds of the mail ships, and its steamers were more comfortable in a rough sea. However, when things were really bad outside, the ships did not sail. Thus on 17 November 1893 there was no night crossing from Holyhead due to severe gales. At other times the departure of a steamer would be delayed until conditions improved. On 22 December 1894 the night boat did not leave Holyhead until daylight, instead of at 3.00am. There were still some rough passages, however, and on the same day *Banshee*, on the day service, took 9 hours to cross, with damage to the ship being estimated at £115. Fortunately there were no injuries to passengers, although they probably did not much enjoy the passage.

Passengers in 1st Class sometimes caused trouble: they had a habit of jumping overboard, which delayed the ship and upset other passengers. In February 1887 a man went overboard form *Lily* and could not be traced, as he had left only his hat behind. Just a year later, on 28 March 1888, a passenger fell overboard from *Rose*. He was picked up, but 'life was extinct'. On New Year's Day 1898 the wife of one Major Sankey went missing from *Banshee*, and it was assumed that she had done so too; whether she had been celebrating too much or simply could not face a new year was not certain.

Occasionally passengers in 1st Class could be just as troublesome as deck passengers. On 14 July 1889 one Mr Johnston assaulted the ticket collector and second mate of *Banshee*, for which he was later fined £2 in court; the cause of the disagreement was not recorded. More alarming, given that Ireland was then in a state of unrest, was the passenger who crossed in *Rose* to Dublin on 17 October 1882 carrying dynamite. He was arrested on arrival but later released, as it was found that he was carrying the material for a legitimate purpose. A cattle dealer, J. MacCormack, became violent when on passage to Dublin aboard *Violet* on 7 October 1893 and had to be locked up in a spare room. He then tried to knock the door to pieces, and when he arrived he was handed over to the Dublin Metropolitan Police and was in due course fined £3 plus £1 damages. By contrast, no serious incidents were recorded concerning steerage passengers.

However, the latter did on occasion cause trouble in another way. In 1890 two letters were received from passengers who had occasion to complain about the Greenore ships' deficiencies in steerage. One was from a Mr Gorton, whose party had been so disgusted that they had returned from Ireland by a different route, at an additional cost of £2 10s. The other was from a Mrs Read, who had had to pay 7s 6d to have a cabin. Admiral Dent explained to the Traffic Committee (the recipients) that it was difficult to provide seats on the steerage deck, as they would interfere with the arrangements for cattle. The Locomotive Committee and the General Manager were asked to consider the matter, but it would appear that nothing was done, beyond a reduction in the charge for cabins. Later, in March 1893, another dissatisfied Greenore passenger had the temerity to write to the Board of Trade, with which the LNWR was generally not on very good terms in any case, to complain of the facilities offered to steerage passengers. Apparently the deck shelter had been used for cattle. The matter was deferred for further consideration and it is not clear what reply was ultimately sent. However, in 1897 the charge for cabins on ships other than the express steamers was reduced from 5s 6d for passengers and 1 shilling for dealers to 1 shilling for all, and the new Greenore steamers were given covered accommodation, available free to all steerage passengers.

Even as far back as the 1850s the Chester & Holyhead Railway had actively encouraged labourers going over to Britain as harvesters to use its services, and stationed agents, who could speak Gaelige, on the platforms at the Midland & Great Western Railway's Broadstone station in Dublin, the arrival point of most of these men in the city. By the 1880s thousands travelled by LNWR cargo ships every year, usually in the summer and autumn months, and they were inclined to cause problems. On 26 February 1892 *Duchess of Sutherland* came over from North Wall with 263 harvestmen on board and en route three stole a box of salmon, for which each received eight days imprisonment. In 1893 another was caught stealing salmon and was fined 20 shillings, with the option of 14 days inside. On the return journey, flush with money, they often celebrated well rather than wisely, and in October 1891 one James Carney, who had been observed to be drunk, fell overboard from *North Wall* in Holyhead harbour. He drowned and a petition for compensation from his widow was declined. But perhaps some took to drink to numb them against the effects of the passage, in wretched conditions.

On 26 October 1887 *Alexandra* shipped a heavy sea off the South Stack, causing serious injury to two harvesters and killing a third. He was one John Fleming, and had stowed away in the horse stalls, where a bulkhead fell on him. His widow petitioned the LNWR for some consideration but the company declined. On 19 October 1896 a harvester died of heart disease on board *Olga* en route to Dublin, and at the inquest it was revealed that there were 300 on board, although she had no facilities for passengers. They were no doubt glad to disembark when they reached port. In July 1887 a harvestman travelling on board *North Wall* had his leg broken in the crush to go ashore at Holyhead. He was treated at the company's expense in the local Stanley Hospital, rather than in the workhouse, suggesting that the LNWR accepted some responsibility.

Accidents such as this involved in the first instance a Holyhead doctor. In the 1880s this was Dr O. Williams, and in the 1890s Dr Hughes, who seems to have been regarded as an unofficial medical officer to the company. Generally he gave good service, perhaps too much so on occasion. In November 1895 he had to ask for more money, arising from his attendance on men who had sent for him without first seeking authorisation. Captain Binney reported to the Locomotive Committee that these were non-urgent cases and the good doctor was told to look to the patients for his money. The eyesight of commanders and officers was tested every two years, and for this Dr Hughes received 5 shillings per man. He must have had a secure income from his other patients in Holyhead, since it is doubtful if he could have made a living from the LNWR. The company also paid an annual subsidy of £5 to the Stanley Hospital at Holyhead, on the understanding that it would treat any of the company's servants who met with a severe accident, these last two words being underlined.

In those days there was a substantial British garrison in Ireland and soldiers were constantly travelling to and fro, often on LNWR ships. They could also be troublesome. On 23 September 1882 37 men of the Shropshire Regiment crossed from Dublin on *Rose* and were 'exceedingly unruly'. One was detained at Holyhead to allow the captain to take court action, and in due course he was given 14 days in prison to cool off; the company was not best pleased that it had to pay 9 shillings in costs. Soldiers continued to cause trouble from time to time, and in June 1890 the Board instructed Admiral Dent to write to the War Office suggesting that the travel warrants should be made out for passage by the cargo boats. In reply, in September 1890, the company was informed that the terms of its contract with the War Office would not allow it to do so. Where there were soldiers, there would also be deserters, and on 16 September 1887 a passenger to Greenore on board *Eleanor* realised that his watch had been stolen. The captain instituted a search and it was found on one John Burns, a deserter, who was in (clearly ineffective) custody. Dundalk magistrates sentenced him to six months hard labour.

Inevitably the LNWR's ships became involved in rescue work from time to time and, when the law of the sea came into play, shore rivalries were forgotten. LNWR ships would always help CDSPC ships if these seemed to be in trouble, as on 15 January 1891 when *Violet* accompanied the mail boat into Holyhead after the latter had suffered a (rare) breakdown. Other vessels were rescued from time to time, but on one occasion in 1886 the Board members were annoyed to find that, after *Eleanor*, on passage from Greenore, had rescued the SS *Shannon* and towed her back to that port, with a consequent delay to her own schedule, only £25 was offered in compensation by the *Shannon*'s owners. Steps were then taken to secure a better settlement, and in due course £75 was paid over, this being distributed among *Eleanor*'s crew.

Publicity for its shipping formed one of the themes of LNWR cards, and some are illustrated here. The first, a card from the Additional Series of January 1905, shows four Holyhead ships. Clockwise from top left, they are *Cambria*, built for the Chester & Holyhead Railway in 1848; *Violet* at Holyhead; *Cambria* of 1897 on trials on the Firth of Clyde; and the cargo ship *Olga* at Holyhead. *Author's collection*

Sometimes the LNWR managed to convey an impression that it was even more 'premier' than it actually was. This card of the Stranraer steamer *Princess Maud* of 1904 makes no mention at all of the other railways that were partners in the Stranraer-Larne service, leaving the lay purchaser to assume that it was solely an LNWR operation! *Author's collection*

A publicity postcard of the period 1908-14, with one of the 'Cambria' sisters on a tranquil sea. Again the company is somewhat economical with the truth: it was not, in itself, the fastest route to Dublin, and the 'open sea passage 2hrs 45mins' must have excluded the more open part of Dublin Bay, sometimes anything but calm! The 'submarine signals' were presumably echo depth-sounding apparatus. *Author's collection*

Timings of the LNWR services inbound from Ireland in 1906 were:

| | Day express | | Night express | |
	arr	dep	arr	dep
Belfast		7.30am		5.00pm
Sligo		5.50am		3.20pm
North Wall		11.00am		9.20pm
Holyhead	3.00pm	3.15pm	1.40am	2.00am
Euston	8.50pm		7.30am	

Publicity

The LNWR had always maintained a very high standard in its publicity material, although in Victoria times details such as type of print tended towards the florid. However, with the arrival of the picture postcard, the company found a niche that offered even greater scope to its artistic talents, which it exploited to the full. It all began in a rather unlikely manner, when the LNWR had a stand at the Louisiana Purchase centennial exposition in St Louis in 1904 and decided that the new-found medium of the postcard would be an ideal way of spreading its message to a large number of people at minimal cost. From that beginning LNWR postcards took off, and between 1904 and March 1906 4.5 million cards were sold. In one of those comparisons beloved of the Victorians and Edwardians, it was claimed that, if these were piled on one top of the other, they would make a column 7,000 feet high!

Holyhead Hotel

There had been inns, of varying quality, in Holyhead ever since travellers first began to use it as a port for Ireland, and perhaps the most famous of these was the Eagle & Child, the terminus of the mail coach service. In 1821 this was renamed the Royal Hotel, to commemorate the visit by King George IV en route to Ireland, and by the 1840s it was the premier establishment in the town. In June 1851 the Chester & Holyhead Railway took a lease on it for 24 years. To improve matters, the LNWR despatched Mrs L. Hibbert, the manageress of its refreshment rooms at Wolverton, and by 1853 it was recorded that there was 'a plentiful supply of luxurious food'. Mrs Hibbert also ran the omnibus that carried passengers from the original station out to the Admiralty Pier before the railway link was opened in 1859.

However, for its new station the LNWR wanted something much better and the five-storey Station Hotel was opened in 1880. This offered 65 bedrooms and also the convenience of a lift. From the rear of the hotel there was direct access to the arrival and departure berths. In 1906 the average cost of a single room was 4 shillings per night, while a double was 6s 6d. Each room had a washstand, and the beds had curtains that could be drawn round to ward off draughts. A plain breakfast and luncheon each cost 1s 6d, while dinner was 2s 6d to 3 shillings. There was a separate room and separate tariff for commercial gentlemen. Supper could be provided for passengers arriving off the night boats from Dublin and Greenore, no doubt much welcomed by travellers in the small hours.

The LNWR seems to have made a point of employing only 'English' staff in its hotels – though at Holyhead this would not exclude Welsh people – and was not sorry to see this emphasised by the columnist 'Dragonet' in a magazine called *The Reefer* about 1906. By 1950, as the manageress

The Carlingford Lough steamer **Greenore** passes the LNWR hotel in **August 1899.** *London & North Western Railway Society*

sadly recorded, 'the purpose for which this hotel was established no longer exists', as former regular patrons took to air travel, and occupancy rates in the winter of 1949/50 were below 19%. It closed in 1951 and was demolished in 1978/9. After a delay of some years, the present Stena House was built on the site, in a style that harmonises to a fair extent with the station. Ironically the Royal Hotel still exists, being used as houses and an office, and is now a listed building.

To further improve the attractions of Holyhead, Commander Holland, who had replaced Captain Binney as Marine Superintendent in 1907, persuaded the LNWR Board to allow him to lay out a golf course at Treaddur Bay. This was opened in 1912 and proved initially to be most popular. However, with changing times after 1919, it saw fewer visitors and in 1950 was sold to its members. As one of the most beautiful courses in Britain, it is still very much in business today.

The LNWR's enemies

There were enemies, too. Passengers at the time and railway enthusiasts since have tended to take the LNWR at its own valuation – the 'Premier Line'. However, the minutes show that at any given time the company could be fighting a war on several fronts. One enemy was, as mentioned elsewhere, the City of Dublin company. A kind of cold war rumbled on more or less permanently and occasionally flared up into outright hostilities. One of the major battles occurred in March 1886 when there was a collision in Dublin Bay between *Banshee* and the City Company's cargo ship *Kildare*. The LNWR was incensed to receive a bill for £224 16s and the solicitor was instructed to return this with the company's bill in return. As it seemed that no settlement would be possible, the LNWR threatened the other with the House of Lords, and that seems to have been the end of the matter.

The Board of Trade could be very difficult. In 1886, when *Shamrock* was given new boilers, the Board refused to issue a certificate until she had been running for three months, but of course she could not legally run without a certificate. Admiral Dent seems to have managed to deal with this piece of bureaucracy. In 1887 the Board refused to provide fog signalling at Holyhead, although the LNWR was willing to meet half the

cost of £1,648. There was also a battle about the fitting of searchlights to the express steamers; the Board submitted bills for surveys that, the company claimed, had already been paid.

The Dublin Port Board could also be unhelpful, particularly if an LNWR ship had been involved in an accident. When *Shamrock* had a contretemps with a ship named *Jasper* in March 1886, the DP&DB refused to make available certain evidence and, to the LNWR's annoyance, the damages were awarded equally between itself and the owners of the ship.

The Mystery of the Disappearing MP

In November 1888 the LNWR suddenly found itself thrust into the front line of Anglo-Irish politics. The cause of this was the conduct of one Mr Pyne MP, who, the Locomotive Committee noted, supposedly disappeared from *Shamrock* somewhere between Holyhead and Dublin. This took place at a time when a commission was investigating the conduct of Charles S. Parnell, the Irish parliamentary leader, relating particularly to letters that had appeared in *The Times* over his signature and which suggested that he had advocated violence.

Jasper Douglas Pyne was certainly a colourful character who, though born in England, became an ardent supporter of the Irish party and as such sat as MP for Waterford West from 1885 until 1888. He became involved with what was known as the 'Plan of Campaign' – a movement to obtain fair rents for tenant farmers – and was to be arrested under Balfour's Crimes Act following a speech he made. However, he barricaded himself into his home of Lisfinny Castle and for three months managed to make 25 officers of the RIC look singularly foolish as they tried to arrest him. Finally he escaped to England, where he was arrested and sentenced to a prison sentence of 18 weeks. He left prison in October 1888 and on 13 November sent a telegram from Holyhead to a fellow MP, Justin MacCarthy, asking him to meet him in Dublin on the next day. Rather strangely he did not take the mailboat, as Irish MPs normally did – perhaps he did not want to meet any colleagues – but boarded the LNWR steamer. Not long after leaving Holyhead, he appeared to be ill and another passenger suggested that he should go to his cabin and lie down. He did not take this advice, but went out on deck, where he was seen pacing up and down, his hands in his pockets, muttering to himself. He did not show up at Dublin and it seemed that he had been lost at sea. Certain documents allegedly belonging to him were laid before Admiral Dent, who then had to take time off from running his fleet to appear before the Parnell commission.

No definite conclusion could be reached about what had happened to Jasper Pyne. He probably committed suicide, as he was by now bankrupt and living on charity. He may have fallen overboard, but the sea was calm and that would actually have been quite difficult to do. He may have been pushed, perhaps by an aggrieved unionist – though this would have been most unlikely – or by a supporter of one Mr Piggot, an informant and forger, who was about to be unmasked by the above-mentioned commission and may have feared that Pyne would be called to give evidence. Possibly it was all an elaborate hoax to allow him to start again, perhaps abroad, with a new identity.

Whatever the reason for his disappearance, it was rather unwelcome publicity for the Holyhead service.

LNWR crews and shore employees

Within the limits of Victorian management, it would seem that the LNWR managers strove to treat their staff well and as fairly as possible.

Captains were obviously at the top of the tree and enjoyed a good salary, plus a pension on retirement. From 1 January 1894 the scale, for those in the passenger service, ranged from £275 per annum on appointment to £350 after ten years' service. Meals were provided free. There was also a safe navigation bonus of £50 per annum. In the cargo boats, the salaries were £200 and £225 after three years, with a safe navigation bonus of £25. These figures, at least at the upper end of the scale, were above those offered by any other railway company, as the following table shows:

LB&SCR: £208-234 (passenger service); £169-
    182 (cargo service); SN bonus £40
GER: £250-275
LC&DR: £300 plus half the profits on catering
Barrow SN Co: £300

Possibly because of these generous scales, captains stayed with the LNWR for most of their career; in 1893 the four captains in the express service had been with the company for 37, 27, 20 and 20 years respectively, while those in the cargo service had served between 17 and eight years. Ages ranged from 36 to 65.

Chief officers on passenger steamers received £130 per annum, while a chief steward on the express ships had 40 shillings per week and an under-steward 20 shillings; stewards on the Greenore service received slightly less. If a chief officer acted as captain, he received 1 guinea per week above his normal salary.

Engineers also generally had long service. In the autumn of 1894 the 13 chief engineers had service varying between 18 and seven years, the average being just under ten years. Their salary scales were revised from 6 July 1894 and were £172 per annum for a chief engineer, £124 for a second, and £98 for a third engineer in the passenger service. There were increments for long service.

The reference to catering on the LC&DR ships is interesting, and on the LNWR the scales outlined above were brought in from 1 January 1894, when it had been decided that catering should, from that date, be undertaken by the hotels department; until then, captains had received part of the profit, but it is not clear exactly how much. However, the scale of the compensation awarded to the captains – the two most senior, G. Taylor and T. Varian, were given an additional £200 per annum – suggests that catering had been quite profitable! In the first half-year after this change, the profit on catering was £759. For new captains, a safe navigation bonus was introduced, at a rate of £25 in the cargo service and £50 in the passenger service, and in 1895 all commanders qualified for this.

The salaries of the office staff were re-organised at the same time, partly because of the dismissal of R. Reece, the former storekeeper, who had been neglecting his duties. In fact, he had clearly taken advantage of Captain Binney, since he had gone absent without leave in the previous year, but had been re-instated. The office was under the management of W. Hall, chief cashier, who earned £225 per annum. Salaries ranged downwards to that of W. Edwards, clerk, who was on £35 a year. Apprentice clerks received £30.

In the autumn of 1893 Captain W. Johns, aged 47, of *Anglesey* suffered three attacks of what was described as 'cerebral irritation' while on duty. This was diagnosed by Dr Hughes of Holyhead as epilepsy and he was granted three months' sick leave. The Board then decided that he should be retired on superannuation, plus a gratuity of six months' salary. He was replaced by Angus Kerr. Mr Manning, the mate, who had been in temporary command, was granted a bonus of £3 3s 4d. Where possible the company tried to find alternative employment for those who had to retire early from a sea-going post. In July 1894 Mr Williams, a chief officer in the cargo service, had to retire because of bad eyesight and he became a timekeeper at £65 per annum. This generosity even applied to some cases where a breach of discipline had occurred.

Accidents did not necessarily terminate a career, especially with the resources of Crewe Works behind the company. In November 1894 J. Williams, leading stoker on *Banshee* had to have an arm amputated after an accident, the nature of which was not recorded. Mr Webb was asked to supply an artificial arm and, as no mention was made of any alternative employment, it would seem that he resumed stoking. Mr Webb's services were also called in if it was thought that an employee was malingering on sick pay. In he summer of 1896 the Locomotive Committee had clearly run out of patience with seaman William Jones of *Rosstrevor*, who had been in receipt of insurance allowance since injuring his knee a year previously. Mr Webb was asked to supply him with a properly fitting, lacing knee-cap, no doubt to allow him to return to work.

Crews were taken on and dismissed as necessary, always at Holyhead, where what was known as the Shore Gang provided a pool of casual labour. However, it seems that, especially in the passenger service, some remained with the company for many years. Judging by surnames, most were from North Wales, although some were probably Irish. They were not covered by the superannuation fund, but were covered by the company's insurance, provident and pension fund in the event of some accidents. Such was the case of Hugh Jones, coal porter, who met with an accident, of an unspecified nature, in November 1894. He was granted 100 weeks' insurance allowance of 21 shillings per week and a permanent disablement allowance of £100, but no pension.

However, this fund did not cover accidents at sea. On 15 October 1898 quartermaster Evans had an accident and his widow received only £10 from the fund. It must all have been too much for the poor lady as she too died on 21 November. The Locomotive Committee then relented a bit and decided to pay £1 per week to the grandmother who was now bringing up the five children. Others had to go on working until just before they dropped, then seek the company's charity in the matter of a gratuity or pension.

On the whole, it would seem that the LNWR, in a paternalistic kind of way, was not unsympathetic. In July 1893 O. Owens, a labourer, died after an accident at Holyhead and the company supplied a coffin, a not inconsiderable item in funeral expenses at that time. Later in the same year the Locomotive Committee agreed pensions of 5 shillings per week to three men – a quartermaster and two carpenters – all over the age of 70. Perhaps the record went to Joseph Jones, a leading stoker, who had been with the company for 40 years and was 77 in February 1896; he was given a pension of 9 shillings per week and a gratuity of £50 from the provident fund. Considering the amount of coal he must have shovelled in those 40 years, he richly deserved both!

The only employment for women in the service was the post of stewardess, but little is known of these ladies or their conditions of work. The only mention made of them was when there was some breach of discipline. In the autumn of 1888 the stewardess of *Earl Spencer* was dismissed when it was discovered that she had allowed passengers from 3rd Class to transfer to the saloon but had been unable to account for all the money due from them. Much the same fate awaited Miss Hughes, stewardess on *Banshee*. On the night of 1 August 1896 it was necessary to bring the ship into commission unexpectedly; she had been 'strange and defiant' in her manner – perhaps she was tired – so she had to go. From this it appeared that a stewardess earned 12 shillings per week. In May 1893 it was decided that stewardesses should wear uniform.

10. THE LNWR AT GREENORE

As remarked elsewhere, the London & North Western Railway had a habit of turning up in unexpected places, none more so than Greenore. The site of this little port near the mouth of Carlingford Lough offered considerable advantages over Newry, which could be reached only by canal, and, as of 1870, it had no rail connection. The LNWR had already been closely involved with the Irish North Western Railway, which ran from Dundalk westwards to Clones and Enniskillen, and in 1863 that concern discussed the possibility of building a rail link to Greenore from its terminus at Dundalk. From the port, private owners would run ships to, among other places, Holyhead. It seemed an excellent scheme: without any outlay of capital by the LNWR, a new source of traffic would be tapped, and any ambitions held by the Midland Railway – newly installed at Barrow – concerning traffic to and from the north of Ireland would be nipped in the bud. However, the outcome, after much detailed wrangling, was quite the opposite.

The Irish company found it very difficult to raise capital, the private shipping companies showed a distressing lack of interest in the project, and in the end the LNWR actually built and operated the new line. By the LNWR Steam Vessels Act of 1870, it obtained powers to run the ships itself. In 1876 it added a line from Greenore to Newry, and at Greenore the company built a two-berth pier and station. It was on a smaller scale than Holyhead, but the transfer facilities for both passengers and cattle were under cover. Later, in an attempt to create a holiday resort, it added a hotel, several self-catering bungalows, bathing machines and a 12-hole golf course.

The little town was considerably expanded, in a miniature version of Crewe, with English-style terrace houses, a gas works, an RIC station and a school; a power station was added at a later date. Standard LNWR 0-6-0 saddle tank engines and rolling-stock were imported to work the line of what was now called the Dundalk, Newry & Greenore Railway, which was to survive in a time warp until 1951.

In an attempt to improve the somewhat bare appearance of the new settlement, the LNWR also planted a number of trees around the area. These proved to be very appetising for the goats kept by one Mrs MacKivron, widow of a former railwayman, and by 1876 the trees had disappeared. The LNWR board then took time off from more weighty matters such as continuous brakes to discuss the problem, and Mrs MacKivron was firmly instructed to tether her goats. Presumably they ate their way through the ropes, since within 18 months the replacement trees had gone the way of the first planting. She was now told to give up goat-keeping, and that was the end of the matter.

From the point of view of cross-channel traffic, Greenore had several advantages. In co-operation with the Great Northern Railway, a new through route to Belfast could be established, with a shorter sea crossing of around 5 hours and a quicker overall journey than the service via Fleetwood, which the LNWR had to share with the Lancashire & Yorkshire Railway. However, for both passengers and cattle traffic it also offered a much quicker through route to the north-west of Ireland, with its rich pasturelands. At 75 miles, the open sea passage was considerably shorter than that of rival routes. It appeared to have potential to return a good profit on the investment.

The Lord Lieutenant of Ireland, Earl Spencer, agreed to inaugurate the new port on 30 April 1873, 'an event of great importance in the history of the county', according to the *Belfast Newsletter*. There followed a celebration the like of which had not been seen in the area before and would not be seen again. More than 800 guests were invited, and when the Viceroy arrived he was taken for a short cruise on the Lough aboard *Edith*. All went off very well, except that one of the commissioners of Carlingford Lough took advantage of His Excellency's presence to complain vociferously about the withdrawal of their government grant. When they returned, there followed a sumptuous déjeuner, with 30 courses (perhaps it was actually a buffet) and 20 speeches. One of the staff present at the opening was one Paddy McShane, who was also present, aged 97, when the service closed in 1951.

The dignitaries then went home and the LNWR started its service between Holyhead and Greenore, with *Edith* taking the first sailing out of Greenore and *Countess of Erne* that from Holyhead. There was a nightly crossing in each direction and connecting trains at Holyhead. On the Irish side, there was a boat train to Belfast, later complete with breakfast car going north and tea car coming south, and there were also through carriages to Armagh and Derry; those to the former had been withdrawn by 1900. A traveller leaving Euston at 5.10pm could arrive in Belfast at 11 the next morning and Derry at 2.15pm. Two new ships were built for the route, *Eleanor* and *Earl Spencer*.

The service attracted a reasonable amount of traffic, but the expected profits did not materialise; instead, in the 1880s, the railway operation was losing the LNWR about £28,000 per annum, something of the poor relation of the Dublin service. By the beginning of the 1890s it was in the doldrums, and when Captain Binney succeeded Admiral Dent and Frederick Harrison succeeded Sir Richard Moon as Chairman (of both the LNWR and the DN&GR), it was decided that a real attempt should be made to turn it around and attract tourists to it, as well as increased ordinary traffic. In 1895 the LNWR Board concluded a new agreement with the Commissioners of Carlingford Lough, which provided for a payment of £1,500 per annum to cover one sailing in each direction per day. Additional sailings were to be charged at half rate and the agreement was to run for ten years.

A new twin-screw ship was ordered for the service, which was duly launched at Denny's yard on 26 February 1895 as *Rosstrevor*. She had good facilities for cabin passengers, with a dining saloon forward on the main deck, a ladies' lounge and a smoke room, but the most important innovation was the provision of covered accommodation for steerage passengers, no extra charge being made for this. Unfortunately on trial on 15 May she failed to work up to her contract speed and had to go back to Greenock for examination. The Chairman then had an interview with Mr Brock of Denny's and it was decided to bring the ship to Holyhead and put her into service, but not to take delivery. She made her first voyage on 11 June and, before leaving Greenore on the return trip, a cattle dealer was found unconscious at the foot of the stairs leading to the steerage sleeping cabin. He was taken to the hotel and a doctor was called. The company was no doubt relieved to learn that he made favourable progress, but some took it as a bad omen for the new ship.

Not for the first or last time did the LNWR learn that the cost of putting a new ship into service was often greater than that of the vessel herself. The more complex machinery of *Rosstrevor* required the employment of an additional engineer, one E. Hughes, at a salary of £98 per annum. Then the piling at Holyhead had to be altered, at a cost of £750, and the same applied at Greenore, costing £370. More worrying was the need to undertake extra dredging at the latter port, at a total cost of £3,500. Finally, a new crane was required at Greenore, and that cost £630.

A series of model trials in Denny's experimental tank suggested modifications that would give the required speed, and in September she was fitted with new three-bladed bronze propellers. She then just reached her contract speed of 17.5 knots under forced draught. After a further interview with Mr Brock and Mr J. M. Denny, the Chairman recommended that she be accepted and she formally joined the fleet in October. Denny made a loss of £2,339 on the final price of £45,198 for the ship, but the care they took over her problems must have paid off in the long run, since the Board was clearly impressed and further orders followed in due course. On 21 February 1896 it was decided, by a meeting in the Chairman's room, to ask for tenders for a second new ship for the service, and on 17 April the Board accepted Denny's tender of £47,900. She was launched on 7 November 1896 by Lady Stalbridge as *Connemara* and proved to be about 1 knot faster than her sister.

Matters were clearly improving, since in 1898 it was decided that stewards should have their pay increased from 30 shillings per week to either 32 or 34 shillings, in view of the great increase in the number of saloon passengers now using the service. However, the running of two fine new ships alongside one elderly vessel brought criticism from the public, and on 13 August 1897 the Chairman's committee accepted Denny's tender of £51,250 for a third, slightly larger, ship, fitted with quadruple-expansion machinery. Named *Galtee More*, she took up service on 11 August 1898. On 3 December of the same year, nine cattle were lost through injury on board during a singularly bad crossing and a cattle man was also severely injured. This was a most unusual occurrence, bad enough to be brought to the attention of the Goods Committee. Other than by shipwreck or collision, the LNWR prided itself on not losing a single animal.

The LNWR guide book for 1905 enthused about the charms of Greenore as a holiday resort. The golf course had now been enlarged to 18 holes, but tennis and croquet were also available. There was sea and river fishing, bathing and boating, and excursions by (jaunting) car could be made to Kilkeel and Warrenpoint. The local roads were 'no trouble to cyclists'.

The service was by night only, and at this date the outward timings were:

	arr	dep
Euston		7.30pm
Holyhead	1.15am	1.40am
Greenore	6.00am	6.15am
Belfast	7.40am	

A through coach was run to Derry, arriving at 10.05am.

A steamer service had been operated on

Galtee More, the third of the class, in another LNWR official card. *Author's collection*

Carlingford Lough since the LNWR had arrived at Greenore, but by 1895 the ship on it, a former Mersey ferry named *Mersey*, was definitely past her best and the Board of Trade was asking awkward questions. On 11 November 1895 the LNWR Board decided to order a new steamer for the local service, and the tender of £7,900 from J. P. Rennoldson & Company of South Shields was accepted by the Chairman's committee on 20 December. She was to have compound disconnecting engines, as on many tugs built by the firm. The Board decided that she should be named *Greenore*. She should have entered service in September 1896, under the command of William Cunningham at a salary of 28 shillings per week; however, she proved to be unsatisfactory, as she did not steer properly, her draught was too great and her speed was 1.5 knots below contract. She therefore had to go back to her builders, where she was lengthened by 12 feet, and in return for all the trouble £1,000 was deducted from the contract price. These alterations seemed to cure the trouble and she then ran reasonably well until 1921, being renamed *Cloghmore* in 1912 when the new turbine steamer appeared. She sailed to Greencastle

Greenore **working up to a good speed on trials!** *World Ship Society*

several times per day and made one or two trips to Warrenpoint. Hotel guests at Greenore had the privilege of free travel on her, which represented quite a saving, as the fare to Warrenpoint was 1 shilling single and 1s 6d return.

In 1907 the Greenore route offered a journey time of just over 12 hours from London to Belfast, albeit with the discomfort of changing from boat to train or vice versa at Holyhead between 1 and 2 o'clock in the morning. Results were by now sufficiently encouraging to allow the ordering of a new and more luxurious ship for the service, and the handsome two-funnelled *Rathmore* was built by Vickers at Barrow in 1908. Named after Lord Rathmore, an Irish director of the LNWR, she was essentially a scaled-down version of the Holyhead express steamers, still with reciprocating engines. On the promenade deck there were 12 two-berth and four single-berth cabins, as well as a ladies' deck cabin and lounge, which contained 14 berths. There was also a smoke room for 1st Class and, aft, a similar room for steerage passengers, which had rattan seats. Forward on the main deck was the first class dining saloon, with tables for eight diners. Amidships was another ladies' room, again with 14 berths, equipped with a coffee boiler, and five two-berth cabins. On the starboard side was a

Rathmore alongside at Holyhead in 1925 or 1926. *McLean Museum & Art Gallery, Inverclyde Council*

buffet, four two-berth cabins for gentlemen and a gents' bathroom. Aft were a dining saloon for 3rd Class, with only 12 places, a ladies' room and, right in the stern, a general room with a drinking fountain. The lower deck contained 22 two-berth cabins for 1st Class and, aft, a ladies' cabin with 16 berths. There were also one six-, one four- and one two-berth cabins. Ten dealers had a cabin of their own, right in the stern.

From 1914 to 1919 *Rathmore* operated on the Dublin service in place of the express steamers, and during that period, on 14 March 1918, she collided with a troopship. Five lives were lost of the 732 passengers and 50 crew, two destroyers having quickly come to the rescue, and the ship herself was towed back to Dublin the next day. She resumed her normal route after a spell on the Channel Islands service in 1920, but as traffic was declining the LMS transferred her to Heysham in 1925, before passing her on to run between Tilbury and Dunkerque.

An almost identical turbine ship was built as *Greenore* in 1912 and had a similar career, but was broken up on cessation of the Greenore passenger traffic in 1926. In 1912 the steamers made a working profit for the first time, and the DN&GR

was also briefly profitable. Yet another new ship was ordered from Denny in 1914, but due to the war she did not appear, as *Curraghmore*, until 1919. Her name was that of the country seat of the Marquis of Waterford, but times were changing and both the Greenore service and the nobility of the Anglo-Irish ascendancy were soon to find themselves in very much reduced circumstances. In fact, the new vessel was to spend her first few months on the mail service, on charter to the City of Dublin Company. She took the first LNWR-operated 'Irish Mail' service on 28 November 1920 and returned to Greenore in 1921. Her later career was spent at Heysham (qv). She was one of those unfortunate ships that was to spend much of her career on services for which she had not been designed and on which she attracted marked criticism from the public. She also suffered from a steering defect and sometimes showed a marked propensity to steam round in circles, rather than making for port in a more or less straight line.

A passenger who had suffered aboard composed a poem in Welsh, entitled 'Y Flying *Curraghmore*'. Written in 1920, it is from the collection of Mr A. Pritchard of Holyhead, and the following verses are reproduced here with his kind permission (translated from the Welsh by Erin Fòn Jones of the Ucheldre Centre, Holyhead, and adapted by

Curraghmore **approaching the Irish coast.** *World Ship Society*

the author). Unfortunately no one now knows the name of the original author, who modestly signed himself simply 'T. M. O':

'The English and the Irish
And Welsh from all around
Were asking where the Company
Had ever such a ship found.
She did not ride the waves at all
But went straight through every one
Until she hit rock bottom
With the contents of your stomach.

Some threatened in language awful
If they ever reached the shore
They would have the law on the Company
And that without delay.
I heard one shout out loud,
"Such a craft I've never seen.
It's not some new-type destroyer.
It's not a submarine."'

Crews were equally unenthusiastic about her.

In 1923 the partitioned border and its associated customs posts cut right through not only the DN&GR but also the Irish North Western system. For many dealers it was now much simpler to ship cargo and cattle via either Belfast or Dublin and avoid a border crossing, and traffic via Greenore declined. The passenger service was withdrawn in 1926 and the cargo service in 1951. From 1933 the hotel was let by the LMS to the Great Northern Railway, and it finally closed in 1952.

It is doubtful if the LNWR ever made any money out of all its investment in the Greenore service. Much was financed by the issue of debenture stock, and in 1948 the new British Transport Commission found itself saddled with considerable arrears of interest on this. It was written off.

11. CAMBRIA: ANATOMY OF AN EXPRESS STEAMER

Knowing that the City of Dublin Company was about to impress Irish Sea passengers with its quartet of new mail boats, the LNWR decided in 1896 to order one new ship, which could be the prototype of a class of express steamers for the Dublin service. In August 1896 the Board instructed Captain Binney to draw up a specification for a twin-screw ship and to invite tenders. Details of the results of this exercise are not given in the minutes, but it was resolved to accept Denny's tender of £84,250 for a ship capable of 21 knots, having ample initial stability without being unnecessarily stiff, practically free from vibration. The Board decided that she should be named *Cambria*, and as such she was launched on 9 August 1897. Trials were run on the Clyde on

4 and 6 November, different types of propeller blades being tried, and mean speeds were 21.43 and 21.37 knots. She came south on 1 December, and on the 8th made a run to Dublin with the Chairman and press representatives on board. Despite a strong gale she behaved very well, but at Dublin a rope fouled a propeller and the party could not return until the next day. She was placed in service on 15 December.

Passenger accommodation was on three decks, lower, main and awning (promenade). The general specification stated that everything was to be in the best style and equal in design and finish to any of the most recently built channel steamers of the highest class. Steam heating was provided throughout and an electrically driven system of ventilation ensured that the air in the accommodation would be changed six times per hour. Electric lighting was fitted, but in case of failure – there had been problems with the earlier dynamos on some ships – oil lamps were fitted to the bulkheads.

Cambria glides into the arrival berth at Holyhead while working on the day express sailing from Dublin at a date early in the 1900s. In the left distance the City Company's mail boat can be seen awaiting departure, while on the right is the forepart of *Banshee*, by this time reserve steamer. *McLean Museum & Art Gallery, Inverclyde Council*

Above An LNWR official card of *Hibernia* leaving North Wall on the day express. A table on the reverse gives the through times from London to Irish provincial cities. *Author's collection*

Below *Scotia* in the departure berth at Holyhead before the First World War. *Courtesy of National Library of Ireland*

Right Another LNWR card, this time of *Anglia.* *Author's collection*

Below *Anglia* comes alongside the arrival berth in the 1900s. A couple of cargo steamers are in the background, and a train of LNWR bogie coaches already awaits the passengers. *National Railway Museum*

On the lower deck forward were two sleeping cabins for passengers in 1st Class, one for ladies but easily convertible for use by gentlemen. Forward of these was a cabin for those in 3rd Class, and forward of that again, right in the bow, was a cabin for 12 seamen and firemen, with two-tier berths. Aft was a general cabin for those in 3rd Class, with a small cabin for 'females' and, adjacent to this, a room for 12 under-stewards and cooks.

The main deck had a small parcels room forward, then aft of this was the 1st Class dining saloon. This seated about 80 people on revolving chairs, with sofas around the sides. The sides and ends of the bulkheads were in oak or teak, otherwise yellow pine woodwork was fitted. The sideboards had marble tops, there were 'handsome' mirrors and an English eight-day clock. Cooking

was done on a coal-fired range and, from the inventory of cooking utensils, it would seem that roasts of one kind or another formed the staple fare on offer. A separate galley for the crew was in the forecastle. Aft on the port side was another ladies' cabin, with a bookcase, armchairs and a 'handsome' couch. There were some two-berth cabins aft of this and also on the starboard side, with ladies' and gentlemen's lavatories. These had tiled floors and, in the case of the latter, delft urinals. What were called the 'dressing tables' had marble tops and tip-up wash-basins.

Steerage passengers, who occupied the accommodation aft on that deck, had to make do with cement floors in the lavatories and, in the case of the 'males', enamelled iron urinals. In the steerage general room there was sparred seating

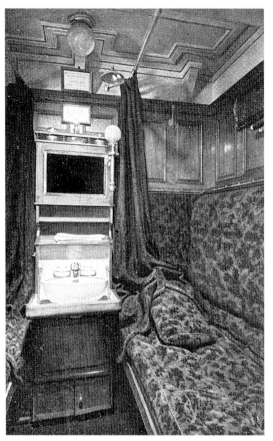

A 1st Class cabin on *Cambria*. The design seems to have been inspired by contemporary railway carriages! *Author's collection*

with dividing armrests, and the floor was covered by linoleum. Three tables were provided and there was a fresh-water drinking fountain. On each deck in steerage there was a combined pantry and bar, equipped with a coffee boiler. If Spartan, it was a great deal better than anything that had gone before, far superior to what would be offered for many years to come on ships of other operators, and, above all, there was no smell of cattle to make the passengers queasy.

On the awning deck were 11 two- or three-berth cabins, forward of the entrance and finished in hardwood and yellow pine. Each cabin had a washstand with a cold water tap and a hardwood locker for 'chamber utensils'. Electric bells were fitted, as was electric light, with shaded candle lamps as a back-up, and the floor was covered with the best five-frame Brussels carpet. Stewards had plenty of accessories, including three best-quality hat brushes, to ensure that they could give appropriate service to those in 1st Class. Further aft in the deckhouse there was a rather small

The smoking cabin of *Scotia*. *Author's collection*

The dining saloon of *Cambria*. *Author's collection*

Hibernia in dry dock, showing the graceful hull lines of these steamers. *G. Rowlands collection*

smoke room, with seats covered in best Morocco leather and circular marble-topped tables. Aft of this were ladies' and gentlemen's cabins. In all the ship could take 230 1st Class passengers and 770 in steerage. When loaded to capacity, the latter must have been very crowded, and perhaps 1st Class was too, since a minute of 1897 refers to the practice of making up berths on the floor of the ladies' cabin on the express steamers at busy times. The figure given above includes berths made up in the dining saloon.

Cambria and her sisters *Anglia*, *Hibernia* and *Scotia* were successful ships. Between 15 December 1897 and 30 April 1906 she steamed 170,946

nautical miles on 2,695 trips without missing a single voyage. In so doing she carried 543,499 passengers, an average of 201 per trip. The busiest period was in the summer months when she carried 11,390, an average of 380 per voyage. To put this in a present-day perspective, it may be compared with the record of the high-speed craft HSS *Stena Explorer*, which in the ten years from 1997 to 2006 made 25,000 trips between Holyhead and Dun Laoghaire, travelling almost 1.5 million miles and carrying 12 million passengers, 2.5 million cars and more than 4,000 units of freight. *Cambria* had a successful war record and, renamed *Arvonia* in 1920, lasted until broken up in 1925.

12. THE 'IRISH MAIL'

Regular postal communication between London and Dublin dated back to 1572 and in the following year this was routed via Holyhead. The Act of Union of 1801 greatly increased the importance of the postal service, since the efficient working of the union depended on regular and reliable communication. It also ensured that Irish MPs would take a close interest in the mail service, since they needed it to keep in touch with their constituents, and they also used the service when travelling between Ireland and Westminster.

In these days of instant communication by e-mail, fax and mobile phone, it is very hard to appreciate the importance and prestige that was attached to mail trains and the ships that connected with them. Of these, none had a greater reputation than the 'Irish Mail', which made its first run on 1 August 1848. It then left Euston at 8.45pm and arrived at Holyhead at 6.45am. The mail packet, at that time operated by the Admiralty, sailed as soon as the mails and passengers had been transferred, and arrived at Kingstown about 5 hours later. All being well, mail posted in London the previous evening would be delivered in Dublin from midday onwards and would reach provincial cities in the late afternoon. Only 11 years earlier, the journey had taken almost 30 hours. There was also a day service operated by the four steamers of the Chester & Holyhead Railway, each of which bore the name of one of the then constituent countries of the United Kingdom – *Anglia*, *Scotia*, *Hibernia*, and *Cambria*. In 1850 the Admiralty's contract was terminated and the new contract was awarded to the City of Dublin Steam Packet Company, a considerable blow for the C&HR, which had also tendered, and the start of a rivalry that was to last for 70 years.

Users were not totally satisfied with the service offered and, after a good deal of discussion, a new contract was signed on 3 January 1859, still with the CDSP company for the sea journey. On 10 August of the same year, the railway line at Holyhead was extended from the station to the Admiralty Pier – from which the mailboats left – over a somewhat precarious wooden bridge, replaced by an iron structure in 1881. These bridges and the tight curves of the line made it necessary to replace the main-line engine by a small tank locomotive for the last part of the journey; apart from a commemorative arch recording King George IV's departure for Ireland in 1821, this pier had nothing to commend it to the passenger. A wooden station was constructed, with a roof covering about half the length of the platform, but this did not extend to the edge of the Pier and passengers had to brave the elements to board the waiting steamer. The new contract provided for a payment to the CDSP of £85,900 per annum, subject to a deduction of half the receipts from passengers if these rose above £3,500. The London-Kingstown time came down to 11 hours, with a crossing time of 3 hours 45 minutes and a penalty of £1 14s for every minute's delay.

To work the new service, the CDSP acquired four ships, which represented a complete step-change in the design of cross-channel vessels. They were named after the four provinces of Ireland, that of *Connaught* being in the anglicised form. They were long, at 334 feet, very slim, with a beam of 35 feet, and their gross tonnage was 1,421. Simple oscillating engines, fired by eight boilers, required an engine room staff of 18, and there must have been about the same number of firemen. The amount of coal consumed per passage must have been enormous.

The ships had a distinctive appearance, since *Connaught*, *Leinster* and possibly *Munster* originally had four funnels. Passengers, almost all 1st Class, were accommodated aft on the lower deck, where

The rather rudimentary facilities on the Admiralty Pier can be seen in this view of *Munster* (1897) coming alongside. *G. Rowlands collection*

the saloon and cabins were stated to be 'lofty and well-ventilated'. The saloon was actually 60 feet long and 9ft 6in high. Postal workers were accommodated forward. Very soon after they entered service, the first three ships were given a

Two of the 1860 quartet alongside Carlisle Pier, Kingstown, at an early date. Forecastles have been fitted, but otherwise the vessels are in original condition. The decorative scrollwork on the bow suggests that the ship on the right is *Leinster*, but this cannot be confirmed. The enormous size of the paddle boxes is readily apparent. In the rather basic train shed, two of the Dublin, Wicklow & Wexford Railway's 2-2-2 well-tank engines await departure. *Courtesy of National Library of Ireland*

long turtle-back forecastle to provide additional shelter when they were being driven hard into a sea, while *Connaught* had this feature from new. Despite their power, they were not able to complete every passage in the stipulated time, the average time over the period 1 October 1860 to 31 December 1882 being 4 hours 7 minutes. This of course included a few very long delays, due to fog, collisions (three), groundings (two) and mechanical breakdown (16). But there was no loss of life and no loss of a single mailbag during this period. It was an impressive record, and at times the steamers arrived at the piers with funnels glowing hot with the effort of keeping the schedule.

The London-Dublin timetable for 1875 was as follows:

	arr	dep	arr	dep
London				
Euston		7.15am		8.30pm
Holyhead	1.50pm		3.05am	
Kingstown	5.50pm		7.05am	
Dublin				
(Westland				
Row)	6.20pm		7.35am	

As stated elsewhere, a new contract was awarded to the Dublin Company on 1 August 1883, to operate from 1 October 1885. Instead of ordering a new fleet to work this accelerated service, the CDSP decided to have one new ship and to rebuild the existing four. The reason given was

lack of time, but it may be that this was an excuse to cover lack of finance, since Denny and other shipyards were fully capable of turning out a high-class cross-channel ship in less than 18 months. Nor has there ever been any suggestion that enquiries were made of shipbuilders. At all events, the new *Ireland* was delivered by Laird Brothers in August 1885 and the other four were rebuilt, with new boilers, modified engines and greatly improved facilities for both passengers and mail workers, of whom there could be up to 30 on board on busy crossings. The new accommodation for passengers, consisting mainly of additional cabins, was contained in a long poop deck, which also afforded better, though still minimal, facilities for those in steerage. All ships now had only two funnels. Thus rejuvenated, the four sisters returned to service and from 1 October 1885 to 31

The paddle steamer *Leinster*, as modified in 1885, comes alongside the Admiralty Pier at Holyhead. *McLean Museum & Art Gallery, Inverclyde Council*

Munster, after rebuilding, lies among the yachts in Kingstown harbour. She is stand-by ship, and the vessel in the background, about to take a service departure, is thought to be *Leinster*. *Author's collection*

Munster of 1897 in the Mersey.
Courtesy of National Museums Liverpool,
Merseyside Maritime Museum

December 1896 the average passage time came down to 3 hours 37 minutes. Not a single passage was missed during this period and there were no collisions or strandings, but there were eight very long passages due to mechanical breakdown. It was an impressive record, but it was totally uneconomical to work the service in this way, with five coal-hungry paddle steamers, and it is doubtful if the CDSP actually made much money out of it.

However, users on both sides of the Irish Sea still wanted something better, and in 1895 the existing contract was terminated and a new one, at £84,000 per annum, was awarded to the CDSP, the LNWR not tendering on this occasion. This time there was no question of making do with existing tonnage, and an order went to Laird Brothers for four new twin-screw ships, which would represent the state of the art in cross-channel ship design. Again they carried the names of the four provinces. The cost of each was £95,905 and they were all exact sisters. Hulls were of mild steel and the ships exceeded their contract speed of 23 knots by 1 knot.

Internally they were a distinct improvement on the paddle steamers. For passengers in 1st Class there were cabins fore and aft on the lower deck, and further cabins amidships on the main deck. Forward on this deck was a very handsome dining saloon, entered by doors decorated with engraved glass and having seating for 80; it was panelled in mahogany in a Sheraton style and boasted a coal fire. The galley was on the upper deck, connected to the saloon by a lift. On the

upper deck there was a 'cosy smoke room' panelled in oak and decorated in a Jacobean style. In the deckhouse aft of this there was a ladies' sitting room, painted white and gold and furnished in a Louis XVI style. Steerage was aft on the main and lower decks and, though not quite as spacious as on the LNWR ships, it was a good deal better than on the old mail boats. The unusually great height between decks – that between main and upper deck was more than 8 feet – combined with an excellent system of ventilation, made the on-board atmosphere a great deal more salubrious than on many other channel steamers. Postal employees worked on the main and lower decks right forward. Again the provision of a high turtle-back forecastle allowed the ships to be driven at full speed into a head sea, but their ratio of 1 to 9 beam to length, combined with their height, made them notorious rollers.

On her maiden voyage, *Leinster* crossed from the end of the breakwater at Holyhead to that at Kingstown in 2 hours 24 minutes, a record that was not broken until the arrival of the high-speed craft a century later. Of course the price for such speed was some extremely uncomfortable crossings, and the postal workers in particular must have suffered the most unpleasant conditions. In service the four ships performed very well and established a record for supreme reliability. However, it must be remembered that only two were in service at any one time, with one on stand-by and one off for repair, and, in comparison to today's ferries, they were distinctly pampered!

Timings from London were, from 1898:

	arr	dep	arr	dep
London				
Euston		8.30am		8.45pm
Holyhead	2.05pm		2.17am	
Kingstown	5.00pm		5.30am	
Dublin				
(Westland				
Row)	5.30pm		6.00am	

These timings remained unchanged up to 1914.

Apart form the arrival of the LNWR day steamers at Kingstown in 1908, all went very well until 1913, when the CDSP Company became involved in the labour disputes that were then racking Ireland. This is not the place to go into the details of such events, but one of their effects was to cause a rift between the company and James Larkin, and it thus lost a powerful ally who might have been able to help it in the troubled years ahead. Nor is there any need to go into the details of the sinking of *Leinster* by UB123, under the command of Captain Robert Ramm, on the morning of 10 October 1918; this has been amply covered elsewhere. But together with the sinking of *Connaught* on active service in 1917, it spelled the end for the City Company. After the war *Ulster* and *Munster* carried on as best they could, with occasional chartered help from their old rival, but they were badly run down and beginning to show their age. The last crossings were made on 27 November 1920, and the officers wore dress uniform to mark the occasion. *Munster* brought over the last mails form Holyhead, and *Ulster* took

the last departure from Kingstown, on which, despite her age and condition, she managed to cross in just under 3 hours.

The ships were then laid up at Holyhead and there was some interest shown by a company that had ideas of using them to challenge the Isle of Man Company, but this came to nothing. It was perhaps just as well, since elderly high-speed ships, with limited saloon space and a huge appetite for coal – the 'Provinces' consumed between 41 and 50 tons on a round trip between Holyhead and Kingstown – were not what the Isle of Man trade required. They were finally broken up in Germany in 1924.

Having finally secured the coveted contract in 1920 (see Chapter 9), the LNWR and, from 1923, the LMS made great efforts to offer a quality service. The new quartet of ships, carrying the same names as those they replaced, went into service between 1920 and 1922, but the LMS soon realised that the lavish provision of four ships was no longer necessary, and *Anglia* was laid up from 1924 and scrapped in 1935. It is not clear why she was chosen for such a short career, but she had been internally much knocked about during a wartime conversion to a minelayer – a process not completed by November 1918 – and her subsequent re-conversion to civilian duties. It is possible that this had weakened her hull. Built during a period of inflation, the final cost of each ship was in the region of £400,000, as against an original contract price of £160,000. They were much faster than previous LNWR ships, being capable of more than 24 knots

The new ships were handsome, perhaps the

Departure of Mail Boat, Kingstown

The ill-fated *Leinster* leaving Kingstown before 1914. *Author's collection*

Top Scotia in original condition: she was called up for war service in December 1939 and made one very successful trip to Dunkirk, when she rescued about 3,000 British troops. Among them was a doctor who had had several bad passages on board the ship, to the extent that he felt sick if he even saw her. However, as he waited to board her at Dunkirk on 29 May, his feelings were just one of pure relief! Her second trip was not so lucky, as she was attacked on her return journey on 1 June, when carrying 2,000 French troops. More than 200 were lost, together with 28 members of her crew. Captain Hughes was the last to leave the sinking ship and for his bravery was awarded the DSC. *Author's collection*

Middle Scotia on the Clyde in April 1932. She is on trials after the alterations to the promenade and upper decks. *Glasgow University Archives*

Bottom Anglia in Dun Laoghaire harbour. She has the tricolour funnels of the period 1923/4, but the original photograph may have been doctored to show these. There is a British destroyer in the left background, and it is most unlikely that a Royal Navy ship would still be using the port by 1923. *Author's collection*

Mail Boat.

most handsome cross-channel vessels ever. In layout they closely followed their predecessors, but they had a lounge forward on the promenade deck. This had 'the comfort of a sitting room, combined with the quick service of a tea room, while its taste is that of a drawing room', according to LMS publicity. The public rooms were decorated by G. A. Crawley, a firm of London architects, in a style that was fairly heavy and in line with such rooms in a hotel on shore. In 1931/2 the three remaining

ships were extensively modernised and given observation lounges under the bridge as well as screening on the forward part of the promenade deck.

They were to have been replaced by new turbine ships in 1940, but this order was cancelled, and from June 1940 *Cambria* and *Hibernia* struggled manfully on, coping with crowds travelling to and from Ireland under wartime conditions. Fortunately the submarine war in the Irish Sea was not repeated, but there were air attacks, one on *Cambria* on 19 December 1940 (other sources give 1941). She beat off the raider with her own armament, but her third officer was fatally wounded. Holyhead was also subject to several air raids, but fortunately there was no loss of life and no serious damage to railway or marine installations. By the end of the war the ships were very run-down, and in July 1945 *Hibernia* quietly sprang a leak and settled down on the bottom in Holyhead harbour, her plates worn paper-thin by years of neglect. This was a distinct embarrassment for the LMS, and of course she was quickly repaired, but an order was placed for two new ships and the veterans were retired in 1948.

Left A link with stagecoach days that was maintained until 1939 was the practice of sending a chronometer from the GPO in London to the Post Office at Holyhead. It travelled in the Travelling Post Office carriage on the train and, as seen here, was carefully handed over at Holyhead. *National Railway Museum*

Below *Hibernia,* as altered. She is presumably relieving on the Belfast service. *Lancaster City Museums*

Above **Cambria** entering Dun Laoghaire harbour. *National Maritime Museum*

Right **Cambria** is taking coal from the coal barge *Herald* at Holyhead in 1933. When the operation is finished, she will be warped over to the departure berth on the left. *W. B. Stocks, courtesy of London & North Western Railway Society*

Timings from London in 1939 were as follows:

	arr	dep	arr	dep
London				
Euston		8.45am		8.45pm
Holyhead	2.05pm		2.25am	
Dun				
Laoghaire	5.25pm		6.00am	
Dublin				
(Westland				
Row)	6.00pm		6.30am	

The new mail boats arrived in late 1948 and were named *Cambria* and *Hibernia*. They were much larger than anything else on the Irish Sea and were the first to be fitted with stabilisers, while diesel engines were another novelty for Holyhead. All 1st Class passenger accommodation was amidships and the standard in both classes was good, but in the matter of space allotted to 3rd Class, they harked back to the 1930s.

In 1964/5 the pair were extensively modernised and a good deal of the 1st Class accommodation was made over to 3rd. Now every passenger in each class could at last count on having a seat under cover. As no day service was now given during much of the year, and as crossing times had been eased, the ships had a fairly leisurely existence for most of their lives; however, when not in service they were often opened to the public at Holyhead at a charge of 1 shilling, and afternoon tea was served aboard, price 2s 6d.

Another feature of those relaxed times was that British Railways put on a new titled train, the

Above Cambria of 1948 at Carlisle Pier, Dun Laoghaire, on 7 September 1949. *Author's collection*

Below The launch of *Hibernia* at Belfast on 22 July 1948. G. *Rowlands collection*

Below Princess Maud at Holyhead in June 1965, with *Hibernia* in the left foreground. In view of the short time that she was to remain in service, it had been not thought worth while to give her the new BR corporate shipping livery. *Author*

Above *Hibernia* leaving Heysham on the 13.45 sailing to Dun Laoghaire on 28 July 1970. *T. J. Edgington*

Below The launch of *St Columba* at Aalborg, Denmark, on 17 July 1976. Her sponsor was Mrs J. Kirby, wife of the then Managing Director of Sealink. One of the Danish Railways' ferries can be seen on the right. *G. Rowlands collection*

In the livery of Sealink British Ferries, *St Columba* enters Dun Laoghaire harbour in May 1990. The last ship built for the 'Irish Mail' service, despite some initial teething problems, soon became a favourite with the travelling public. She became a one-class ship in 1982 and, after privatisation of the Sealink fleet, became successively *Stena Hibernia* then *Stena Adventurer*. In 1996 she was transferred to the Stranraer-Belfast service, thus severing the last link with the days of the mail service. *Author*

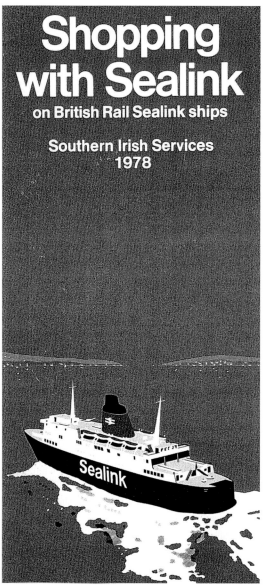

'Emerald Isle Express', which left Euston at 5.15pm and reached Holyhead at 10.30, allowing a good night's sleep on board and at last avoiding the transfer from train to ship in the small hours.

The two ships were worked much harder in the last years of their lives, particularly when the mail service had to be operated from Heysham, due to the fire on the Menai Bridge on 23 May 1970. The sea crossing now took 7½ hours and this schedule had to be maintained until 31 January 1972. They were finally withdrawn in 1974 and were sold to Saudi Arabian owners, being replaced by the magnificent new *St Columba*, built at Aalborg in Denmark. With a nominal passenger capacity of 2,400, she was the largest ferry on the Irish Sea to date and this had considerable implications in the internal design and the provision of life-saving equipment. A casino in the 2nd Class bar and a disco were new features.

A folder listing all the bargains to be had from duty-free goods. This service began in 1978 when the Irish pound and the pound sterling went their separate ways and Sealink was not slow to take advantage of the opportunity. On *Duke of Lancaster* a 1st Class cabin was converted to a makeshift shop, buyers having to queue in the corridor, while on *St Columba* a small shop was created. Business rapidly outstripped these facilities and they were replaced by larger premises when the ship was converted to the one-class layout in 1982. *Author's collection*

13. RAILWAY CARGO BOATS

The original London & North Western Railway ships were built for mixed traffic, in that they carried passengers, cargo and, in some cases, cattle. In the late 1870s it was realised that this did not provide the best facilities for passengers, especially those in 1st Class, and in consequence a series of fine express steamers was acquired, beginning with *Rose* and *Shamrock* in 1876. These had only a very limited capacity for parcels and express goods, sparing passengers the noise and smell of the cattle. In 1878 *Edith*, which had most inconveniently sunk in the middle of Holyhead harbour in 1875, was rebuilt as a cattle and cargo vessel only, and was most successful in her new role, sparing the cattle the ordeal of being confined to the sponsons for the crossing. Shortly afterwards it was decided also to build two new ships to this concept, and Admiral Dent was set to work on the detailed design.

The ships were built by R. Duncan of Port Glasgow, steel being supplied from Crewe, as was to become common with LNWR new builds. Admiral Dent paid particular attention to ventilation, and the ships could accommodate about 800 head of cattle on two decks. Given the dithering about machinery for the express steamers that was to follow (qv), it was remarkable that they were fitted with compound machinery from new. The new shore facilities at Holyhead also had special facilities for dealing with this traffic, and members of the wash-down gang cleansed them thoroughly after the landing of each shipment.

The new ships, named *Holyhead* and *North Wall* by a decision of a special committee of November 1882, went into service in July and September 1883 respectively and were an instant success. With a single funnel, two masts and a speed of 15 knots, they set the pattern for the line of handsome and successful cargo ships that would be

built over the next 80 years. They seemed to work well, although at a later date (May 1897) *North Wall* was fitted with bilge keels to reduce rolling, for which she was said to be the worst ship in the fleet.

However, the early success of the venture was short-lived, as on 31 October 1883 *Holyhead* collided with the German barque *Alabama*, which sank almost immediately. The cargo steamer came off not much better, since she also began to sink and was gone in 20 minutes. Fortunately most of the crew, the four passengers and the seven rescued from the barque were able to take to the boats before she went down. After about 20 hours at sea they were rescued and landed at Holyhead by the schooner *Gertrude* of Caernarfon. No immediate replacement was made, but in 1885 a new vessel, *Irene*, slightly larger and with room for 900 head of cattle, was built by Harland & Wolff and named after the daughter of Admiral Dent.

On 17 November 1886 a meeting in the Chairman's room considered tenders from Harland & Wolff and Laird Bros for new cargo ships. As these were virtually the same, one order went to each builder, at £32,000, and the meeting decided to pay the extra £1,000/£1,200 for triple-expansion machinery. The ships were named *Olga* and *Anglesey*, the latter originally being spelled 'Anglesea'. When the six months' guarantee on the former ended, she was reported to be 'very satisfactory'.

Two older ships, *Duchess of Sutherland* and *Edith*, were converted from paddle to screw propulsion in 1888 and 1892 respectively, the former retaining her paddle boxes and sponsons and thus having a most unusual appearance. However, they were both successful in their new form and it was now possible to operate a four-ship service, with reliefs running as necessary. The following figures show Dublin cargo service loadings, the nature of the traffic and also the considerable variations from month to month.

	May	June	July
1890			
Horses and bullocks	3,016	1,583	3,237
Sheep and pigs	15,800	15,433	15,303
Merchandise (tons)	9,087	7,923	8,726
1891			
Horses and bullocks	2,001	1,416	3,833
Sheep and pigs	8,967	13,303	22,741
Merchandise (tons)	9,503	9,196	10,239

In 1890 the express steamers also carried between 750 and 860 tons of merchandise in the months in question, but in 1891 the figure was much lower.

Normally three goods services were operated in the outward direction, leaving Holyhead at 2.15am, 4.30pm and 8.05pm, but up to three additional sailings could be provided, as in November 1896 when, because of heavy cattle traffic, six services were operated daily.

There were of course incidents. In 1888 a cargo of yarn on board *Anglesey* caught fire and the blaze was not extinguished for 2 hours. The same problem occurred on the same ship at Dublin on 8

In 1908 the LNWR took delivery of two sister ships from Vickers, Sons & Maxim of Barrow. Named *Slieve Bloom* and *Slieve Gallion*, they were a larger development of earlier steamers and led uneventful lives until *Slieve Bloom* was lost on 31 March 1918, after being struck by a cruiser of the US Navy. Her sister continued in service until 1937, when she was sold for breaking up at Dalmuir on the Clyde. This view shows her at Holyhead. *McLean Museum & Art Gallery, Inverclyde Council*

August 1891, when liquid, spilled on the floor of the hold, was ignited by a hand lamp; this liquid was part of a 'dangerous consignment' from D. Mosley & Son of Manchester. Just 16 days later a similar incident almost occurred on the same ship, and on 2 September a case containing matches was found to be on fire as it was being put on board *Olga*. The company decided to prosecute the senders of these potentially dangerous cargoes, but on 18 March 1892 reversed that decision on policy grounds – presumably it was feared that the publicity surrounding a court case would not be to its advantage.

On 19 November 1893 *North Wall* stood by a disabled Spanish ship until a tug arrived, and for his gallantry Captain Roche was awarded a silver medal and diploma by the Spanish government; he had to wait some time for these, as they were not presented to him, by Captain Clapp RN, until 1 February 1896. Crew members were exposed to temptation at times and in June 1893 three on *North Wall* were dismissed when they were found in the hold, 'information having been followed up'.

Although these ships carried deck passengers, as mentioned elsewhere, they had no accommodation for passengers as such and the LNWR began to consider providing some limited facilities, similar to 3rd Class in the express ships, for use by drovers and cattle dealers, a group of people who were becoming important in bringing traffic to its ships. Accordingly the next two ships to be built, *South Stack* of 1900 and *Snowdon* of 1902, were fitted with some passenger facilities and thus began a tradition that was to continue until the end of the cargo service. A further four

One of the ships built early in the 20th century, most probably *Snowdon*. *London & North Western Railway Society*

vessels to this basic design were built in the years up to 1914, and the fleet was also reinforced by the transfer of *Rosstrevor* and *Connemara* from the Greenore service, these being stripped of their 1st Class accommodation.

On the outbreak of war these two went back to Greenore, but, apart from some trooping service in 1914, all the others remained on station throughout the war and their service must have been of incalculable value in ensuring that the food chain to the home market did not break down altogether. Despite the submarine menace, no ship was lost to them, although *Snowdon* was attacked by a submarine whose torpedo failed to

The buildings of the marine yard form part of the background to this photograph taken from the Turkey Shore. The cargo steamer is *North Wall*, survivor of the original pair of 1883, and the off-duty paddle steamer ahead of her is either *Rose* or *Lily*. The lower part of the sheerlegs crane, which dominated the yard, can be seen over the stern of the paddle steamer. *London & North Western Railway Society*

explode on impact, and in February 1918 *Slieve Bawn* was attacked by a submarine on the surface, but managed to make good her escape. However, on 30 March 1918 *Slieve Bloom* collided with a US destroyer and sank; all her passengers and crew were saved, but 370 cattle and 12 horses were lost.

To replace *Slieve Bloom*, and using the money obtained as compensation for her loss, the LNWR bought what was to be its last new ship, *Slieve Donard*, built by Vickers at Barrow in 1921. She had considerably more passenger accommodation than the earlier steamers and could take 134 in 3rd Class. Because of this she was often used on a sailing from Dublin at midday on Thursdays, which was patronised by many dealers, often known as 'the kings of the cattle market'. Although technically 3rd class, the accommodation was quite comfortable and the company made a speciality of serving an excellent three-course lunch to those gentlemen upon leaving Dublin. Later these sailings were taken by one of the new turbine steamers and *Slieve Donard* was stripped of her accommodation. She lasted until 1954.

After 1923 the LMS attached equal importance

Above *Slieve Bawn* going astern into Heysham harbour. *Lancaster City Museums*

Below *Slieve Bearnagh* in the Firth of Clyde, presumably on **trials.** *M. Walker, Lancaster City Museum*

Top *Slieve Bawn* alongside at North Wall in June 1965. *Author*

Middle *Slieve Donard* of 1921. *McLean Museum & Art Gallery, Inverclyde Council*

Right In 1946/7 the LMS built at Derby ten very successful 2-6-4 tank engines of Class WT for the NCC services, and the Ulster Transport Authority added a further eight in 1949/50. The engines were assembled at Derby, then partially dismantled and taken to Heysham on flat wagons. At Belfast they were mounted on temporary driving wheels and made their way via the harbour lines to York Road for final assembly. In this view No 52 is hoisted aboard *Slieve Bloom* at Heysham. *Lancaster City Museums*

The second *Slieve Donard* approaches Larne on 2 August 1964. *Author*

to the service, and from 1930 onwards placed four new turbine ships on the route, the last two of which, *Slieve League* and *Slieve Bawn*, were capable of 17 knots. These four, together with the 1921 *Slieve Donard*, kept the service running throughout the war, which, fortunately, passed off without any major incident for the cargo fleet. In the 1950s they were adapted to carry containers, and in 1959 they were joined by the new *Slieve Donard*, which still maintained the basic profile but in a more streamlined form. She was the first Holyhead cargo ship to have diesel engines. All the older ships were withdrawn in the 1960s, being replaced by container ships, and *Slieve Donard* became something of a nomad on the Irish Sea, before also being sold in 1976 to owners in Saudi Arabia.

While many other railway companies ran cargo ships, only the LNWR and the LMS operated a fleet that was, technically, the equal of the more famous passenger steamers and which was operated to such a rigorous timetable. For more than 80 years these ships played an essential part in the link between Britain and Ireland, and many on both sides of the Sea mourned their passing.

14. YEARS OF EXPANSION: HEYSHAM AND FISHGUARD

By the beginning of the 20th century the Midland Railway was doing very well, and in just over 30 years had come from being a small provincial system to one of the major companies serving London. On 1 July 1903 it would take over the Belfast & Northern Counties Railway in Ireland and would be able to boast that, thanks to some joint running, its system stretched from Bournemouth to Ballyshannon. But it still lacked one major asset of any self-respecting major British railway, a port of its own. True, it had a toe-hold at Stranraer and it part-owned the ships sailing from Barrow to Belfast and Douglas, but these sailed from facilities owned by the relatively minor Furness Railway, and in any case that port was not well placed to handle traffic from and to London.

The Great Western Railway was, of course, simply the Great Western, already with more than 60 years of tradition behind it, but it had always seemed rather lukewarm about maritime activities and its Irish services in 1900 were confined to a service from what was then New Milford to Waterford.

Both of these companies were annoyed over the years by the way in which the London & North Western Railway managed to have a finger in a considerable number of Irish pies. Its activities at Greenore gave it a much more convenient London-Belfast route than that via Barrow could ever hope to be, it had its own facilities at Dublin, and as the century turned it was becoming closely involved with the Dublin, Wicklow & Wexford Railway, assisting it in its goal of reaching Waterford. This assistance took the form of a loan of £100,000 and the purchase of Waterford Extension stock to the value of £87,000. Presently it would have a seat on the board of that company, a situation that was later to complicate the grouping of Irish railways in 1924. The Great

Western's complacency in South Wales was meanwhile rudely shattered; both it and the Midland came to the conclusion that it was time to improve facilities to gain what they saw as their rightful share of the Irish traffic, and, early in the new century, both did so on the grand scale.

Heysham

In 1896 the Midland obtained an Act of Parliament to allow it to construct a new harbour at Heysham, about 3 miles south of Morecambe, and to link this with its own system in the area. The work involved the building of two long breakwaters and it was not an easy task, but the harbour was completed by 1903 and the new branch railway, which posed no problems at all, had already been opened in 1898. Everything was done on the grand scale and in the most up-to-date manner; the port even had its own power station, as all equipment in it was to be powered by electricity. Naturally there was generous provision for the cattle trade and, to enable the animals to have a rest after what might have been a nasty crossing, a paddock was constructed where they could recuperate. A commodious passenger station, with an island platform, was connected to the quay by overhead walkways, and the whole project cost the company about £3 million. All ships were fitted with wireless telegraphy and a signalling station was built at Heysham for this. The port opened to traffic with the departure to Douglas of the new *Londonderry* on 13 August 1904, and the service to Belfast began on 1 September. Laird Line ships provided services to Dublin and Derry.

To work its services the Midland ordered four ships and, unlike most other railways, it went to separate builders (John Brown, Caird, Denny

Top This view of blasting operations during the construction of the harbour at Heysham gives an idea of the amount of work that had to be undertaken. *Lancaster City Museums*

Middle *Londonderry* sets off on her maiden voyage to Douglas. This card was written on 14 September and addressed to the second engineer on the LNWR's *Anglia* at Dublin North Wall. *Author's collection*

Bottom The Midland Railway was not the only operator of ships from Heysham, since Laird Line also ran services to Derry and Dublin. There were some passengers, until about 1930, but they mainly carried cattle and pigs, and a contemporary shipping enthusiast noted that in September each year thousands of geese crossed from Ireland, to be fattened for Christmas in England. This postcard view shows *Azalea* alongside. She was built in 1878 by A. & J. Inglis in Glasgow and served on most of Laird's routes. She had accommodation for 70 passengers in saloon and this was considerably improved in 1893, when she was also reboilered. She was sold to Greek owners in June 1914 and lasted until 1939. The Heysham-Derry service ended on 12 October 1963. *Author's collection*

and Vickers) for each of its fleet. All were, however, designed by Professor Biles of the University of Glasgow, so had a distinct family resemblance.

Londonderry and *Manxman* were given turbine machinery, but as that form of propulsion was still very new, the Midland hedged its bets by fitting reciprocating engines to *Donegal* and *Antrim*. It had in fact originally been intended to fit this type of machinery to all the ships. 1st Class on the latter two and *Londonderry* was on the main, promenade and upper deck forward of the machinery, while 3rd Class was on the upper and promenade decks aft. There were berths for 174 in 1st Class and 76 in 3rd, some enjoying the luxury of four-berth cabins. The Midland did not charge for berths, except for those in single cabins, which cost 2s 6d. It was hoped that this would end the practice of passengers sleeping in the saloons, except at peak periods. The cost of *Londonderry* was £90,783. *Manxman* was slightly longer and wider and had fewer cabins and more saloon accommodation, as she was primarily intended for daylight services to Douglas.

Right Manxman was by far the best known and the finest of the original Midland Railway Heysham fleet. She was built by what was then Vickers, Sons & Maxim at Barrow, but did not actually sail to the Isle of Man until 1905. Her accommodation for 1st Class passengers consisted of a saloon with buffet and a smoke room on the promenade deck, single and two-berth cabins on the main deck, and a dining saloon on the lower deck, which had tables for six. The two-berth cabins were 6 feet by 7 feet, not allowing a great deal of space per passenger. For those travelling 3rd Class there was an entrance with seating in the after deckhouse on the promenade deck, and a ladies' lounge, a dining saloon with sparred seats and a bar aft on the main deck. There were three four-berth cabins and also some accommodation for drovers. For crew members, there was a large cabin for 18 on the main deck aft of the 3rd Class cabins. This post-1920 view shows her leaving Heysham in the livery of the Isle of Man company. *Lancaster City Museums*

Right A fashionably dressed young lady of 1909 on board *Manxman*. *Lancaster City Museums*

Above **Donegal** ran ashore at Point of Ayre, Isle of Man, in October 1908. Fortunately she was not badly damaged and **Wyvern** was sent across from Heysham to tow her off, which she accomplished on the following day. **Donegal** was torpedoed and sunk while on active service in 1917. *Lancaster City Museums*

Below **Antrim** on trials on the Clyde. *Glasgow University Archives*

The normal method of working the Belfast service was for each of the three steamers to run on it for a month, then lay up at Heysham for 15 days, except at peak periods. Connecting trains, with dining carriages, were laid on from and to St Pancras (departures at 5.00pm and 5.20am). In 1907 a local electric service was laid on to Lancaster, this being the first AC electrification in Britain, and the Heysham power station supplied the current. When running, the Douglas service operated from the island to Heysham in the morning, departing at 8.30am, and back in the afternoon, departing at 3.00pm. Aggressive marketing and cheaper day return fares helped to

stimulate traffic on this service and the Midland cheekily sent the little tug/tender *Wyvern* over to Fleetwood to poach traffic from under the nose of the Isle of Man Company. The latter protested at all this, but had to cut fares in accordance with the new levels.

Of course this service had a particularly busy traffic on summer Saturdays. In 1913 four sailings were provided to Douglas, at 10.00am, 11.30am 3.00pm and 12 midnight, with five return workings at 8.30am, 9.30am, 3.00pm, 4.00pm and late evening. (The spare ship operated light from Heysham in the early morning.) *Duchess of Devonshire* was transferred from Barrow to assist

Right Perhaps the most successful ship built for the Midland Railway was the tug/tender *Wyvern*. She was built by Ferguson of Port Glasgow in 1905 and had a passenger certificate for 230. She towed the steamers off local sandbanks when they grounded (this seems to have been a fairly frequent occurrence) and also guided them into Heysham harbour in foggy weather. In summer she operated twice-daily excursions to Fleetwood and until 1914 cheekily collected passengers for the Isle of Man from under the nose of the IOM company and brought them to Heysham to proceed by a Midland ship to Douglas. During the First World War she was a tender at Scapa Flow and she lasted until 1959, having seen three generations of Irish

steamers at Heysham. In this view, taken in the later 1920s, she is setting off on a local cruise with passengers from a Morecambe holiday camp. *Lancaster City Museums*

Above An earlier view of the ship in Midland Railway colours. Behind her can be seen some of the dredgers and hoppers that played an essential role in keeping the port open. *Author's collection*

Right A fine view of *Duchess of Devonshire* in Midland colours. *Author's collection*

One of the problems of Heysham harbour in the early days was the silting up of the approach channel, and the Midland found it necessary to employ two dredgers, *Laga* (bought from Dutch owners) and *Hessam*, built new in 1906 by Simons of Renfrew. There was also a hopper, *Red Nab*. The operation of this small fleet must have eaten into the profits of the Irish service. This view shows *Hessam* at work. *Lancaster City Museums*

with the Manx traffic and was taken over by the Midland in 1907.

Apart from a grounding by *Donegal* on the Isle of Man in October 1908, all seemed to be going very well, but it is doubtful if the company actually made any money from its investment. Constant dredging was necessary to keep the entrance channel open and a grab dredger and two hopper barges had to be bought for this task. All ships were requisitioned in 1914/5 and *Donegal* was lost in 1917. When the others returned, the Midland declined to buy back *Manxman* from the Admiralty, on the rather spurious grounds that it would be too difficult to refit her for peacetime service. The IOM Company then snapped her up and did just that, so successfully that she ran on its premium services until 1939, when she was called up again. It may be that the Midland had decided that that service, as run in pre-war days with a dedicated ship and heavy peak traffic, was simply uneconomical.

Services did not resume to Belfast until 1920, and in 1928 the LMS replaced the Midland ships

with three fine new steamers built by Denny. At the same time the LMS withdrew from the Isle of Man traffic and the former LNWR service via Fleetwood was closed and all Belfast traffic went via Heysham – perhaps the Midland had a last, posthumous laugh!

The new 'Dukes' (*Lancaster, Rothesay* and *Argyll*) were brilliantly successful in stimulating traffic, to the extent where the former Greenore steamer *Curraghmore* was transferred permanently to Heysham in 1930 and re-named *Duke of Abercorn*. She was only too clearly a stop-gap, and when the Belfast SS Company raised with the LMS the question of her being operated as a one-class ship, at 3rd Class fares, the latter shamefacedly agreed that this was indeed the case, giving as an excuse the very poor steerage accommodation, in which it would not have been wise to confine 3rd Class passengers for a 7-hour voyage. In 1935 a fourth new ship, *Duke of York*, appeared. Still the passenger numbers climbed, and in 1939 *Princess Margaret* came down from Stranraer to assist.

T.S.S. DUKE OF LANCASTER
LONDON MIDLAND & SCOTTISH RAILWAY
HEYSHAM & BELFAST
1928

An official and most attractive card showing *Duke of Lancaster* of 1928. *Author's collection*

Above **Duke of Rothesay** at Belfast in wartime grey paint. *National Maritime Museum*

Right All three of the 1928 sisters did their bit for the war effort, although they were not all on active service for the entire duration of the war. This view shows **Duke of Argyll** as a hospital ship, in which capacity she served from July 1944 to June 1945. *Lancaster City Museums*

Below **Duke of Argyll**'s namesake of 1957 at Belfast in August 1964, with **Ulster Prince** behind. *Author*

Left **Duke of Abercorn** leaves Heysham after alterations to fit her for the Belfast service. She was always very much the poor relation at Heysham and was withdrawn in 1935. *M. Walker, Lancaster City Museums*

Below An official card of **Duke of York** as built. *Author's collection*

Below **Duke of York** was transferred away from Heysham in September 1948, soon after the formation of British Railways, but she occasionally revisited her old haunts, as in this view in 1951. She had by that time lost one of her two funnels. When built in 1935, she was a significant ship in that she introduced vastly improved facilities for those in 3rd Class, which LMS publicity now named 'tourist'. There were 228 berths in cabins in this class, as well as open berths, and in all but small details of furnishing these were the equal of those in 1st. For the first time, also, 3rd Class accommodation spread to the midships section of the ship, instead of being confined to the poop, the 3rd Class lounge and smoke room being both located in the midships structure. Electric bridge telegraphs, roller hatch covers and a radio-telephone installation were also innovative. She had a long career, not being withdrawn until 1963, and she then had a further lease of life in the Mediterranean as the cruise ship *Fantasia*. *Lancaster City Museums*

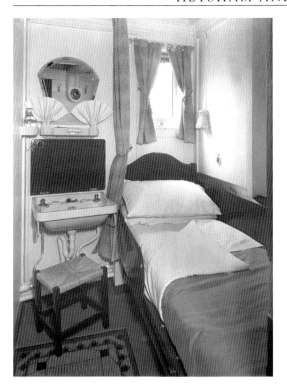

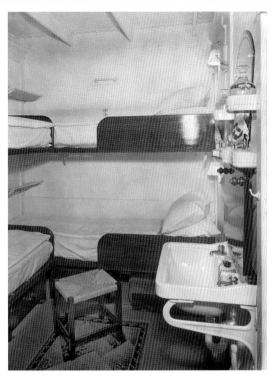

Above Comparison of these two views of cabins shows that the claim of the LMS was not an idle one. In most respects there is little to choose between 1st and 3rd Class, although of course the latter would have been slightly more crowded, with four passengers sharing a relatively small space. *Ulster Folk and Transport Museum*

Below **Duke of York** as **Fantasia**. *Author's collection*

Above The old and the new 'Dukes' at Heysham in 1956. *Lancaster City Museums*

Right and below Publicity for the new ships of 1956/7. *Author's collection*

DUKE OF ROTHESAY *1st class Dining Saloon*

DUKE OF ROTHESAY *2nd class Lounge*

DUKE OF ARGYLL *1st class Lounge*

DUKE OF LANCASTER *De Luxe Cabin*

A NEW ERA IN CROSS-CHANNEL TRAVELLING

LUXURY AFLOAT—that's the best way to describe British Railways overnight service from Heysham to Belfast.

The three new ships: T.S.S. "Duke of Lancaster", T.S.S. "Duke of Argyll", and the T.S.S. "Duke of Rothesay" are superb additions to the British Railways' fleet of steamers. From the moment the passenger walks down the gangway on to the spotlessly clean deck, he knows he's going to have a good trip. Everything is ship-shape and modern. Whilst the traditional features of seagoing steamers are jealously retained, the interior appointments and decor would do justice to a first-class hotel.

The sleeping accommodation has been planned for ease of movement and maximum comfort. The 1st class dining room and the 2nd class cafeteria-combined lounge, are models of superb design and faultless taste. Nothing has been overlooked for the convenience of the passenger. Each cabin possesses a point for electric razors; and, depending on how you prefer the temperature of your cabin, with the flick of a switch you can regulate your personal air purifying outlet from cool to very warm.

Besides the 1st and 2nd class lounges there are comfortable hotel bars. On the 1st class deck a tea dispense is open for passengers who would prefer something lighter than a set meal.

These magnificent ships have the most up-to-date navigational devices available to the Merchant Service. Radar, ship-to-shore contact by radio, wireless telegraphy, even the latest echo-sounding equipment which can pinpoint the distance in feet from the keel of the ship to the sea floor. Not a thing has been left to chance.

In case of bad weather, rolling of the ship is reduced considerably by the incorporation of stabilising fins: fitted for the first time to any ship on the Northern Ireland run—ensuring for the passenger a new ease in cross-channel travelling.

FACTS AND FIGURES

The approximate gross tonnage of the ships averages 4,800. Speed—21 knots. Length overall—about 375'. Length between perpendiculars—354'. Breadth moulded—55'. Depth moulded to main deck—19' 6".

Above Not long before railway steamers ceased to use it, Heysham had the distinction of serving as the English terminal for the 'Irish Mail' service. This view shows *Cambria* leaving on the 13.30 sailing to Dun Laoghaire on 30 August 1970, with the Isle of Man steamer ship *Tynwald* at the quay. *T. J. Edgington*

Below By 1958 the British Transport Commission had realised that there was no future for a cargo service of the traditional kind, and that containerisation was the way forward. Two new ships were built for the Heysham-Belfast route and a new terminal was opened at the latter port. *Author's collection*

Cargo and cattle traffic was booming too, and in 1936 Heysham saw its first cargo ship, *Slieve Bearnagh*. At last the port had fulfilled its potential. This time services were maintained with chartered ships throughout the war, and all the 'Dukes' ultimately returned, though *Duke of York* was soon removed by British Railways in 1948 to fill gaps elsewhere.

Below In this view of Heysham on 30 June 1971 *Container Venture* lies astern of the visiting *Hibernia*. *T. J. Edgington*

Fishguard

From the point of view of the other railway companies in Britain, the London & North Western Railway had an irritating habit of cropping up in places where they least expected to see it, and thus threatening what they regarded as their rightful spheres of influence. It is to this habit that we owe the port of Fishguard in West Wales.

Despite considerable interest in Irish traffic by I. K. Brunel himself, and his creation of the port of Neyland (also known as New Milford from 1860 to 1906), the Great Western Railway had operated cross-channel steamers only from 1872, and then in a very low-key manner. The company began in that year services from Milford Haven to Waterford and Cork, the latter lasting only until 1875, while that to Waterford was moderately successful. About 1884 a small independent company in South Wales proposed building a line to Fishguard from various existing branch lines and offered this to the GWR, which declined to become involved. The promoters then obtained an Act to allow them to connect with the LNWR at Abergwili. The GWR now woke up, acquired the local company and decided to build a line to Fishguard and to become much more seriously involved in cross-channel traffic.

In Ireland the Fishguard & Rosslare Railways & Harbours Company came into existence in 1894, jointly owned by the GWR and the Great Southern & Western Railway to construct a harbour at Rosslare and built connecting lines to Waterford and (further inland) from Fermoy to Cork. When the Dublin, Wicklow & Wexford Railway also came into the picture, with a line to Waterford, the stage was set for new through services via Fishguard to Dublin, Cork and Limerick. The only drawback, from the GWR angle, was that the DW&WR, being chronically short of money, had gone to the LNWR for assistance, and the latter had provided a loan of £100,000 towards the cost of the new line, as well as taking up some shares in it. This was in fact almost half the total cost, and in return the LNWR was granted a seat on the DW&WR Board. This LNWR (and later LMS) presence was in 1924 to complicate the amalgamation of Irish railways, but for the moment it simply annoyed the GWR, which had begun to look on the south of Ireland as its own private fiefdom.

In Wales, construction of the line to Fishguard went ahead, but, as it involved blasting thousands of tons of rock from the cliffs surrounding the bay, it was a slow and expensive process. When space had been cleared, construction of a pier and new goods and passenger stations began. Both these stations were on an impressive scale, that for passengers having two long platforms, allowing travellers to transfer to and from the steamers under cover. At Rosslare a new pier was opened in 1901 and was linked to the mainland by a long viaduct, which contained a railway, a footpath, a cattle run but not, until 1965, a roadway.

All the new facilities, but not the new ships ordered for the route, were ready in the summer of 1906. On 21 July the first crossing from Fishguard was undertaken by *Pembroke*, a modest though handsome little ship that had originally been built as a paddle steamer by Laird Brothers of Birkenhead in 1880. She had been converted to screw propulsion in 1895 and had survived a stranding on Little Saltees Island in 1898. She now had her hour of glory: she crossed over to Rosslare and was welcomed by Lord Aberdeen, Lord Lieutenant of Ireland. Unfortunately Lord Aberdeen was sometimes accident-prone on official occasions and this was to be no exception, as his yacht ran aground. However, she was soon freed and was able to come into the harbour.

The official opening of the new service followed on 30 August. Steamers left Fishguard at 2.15am and 2.15pm, and Rosslare at 11.30am and 11.30pm, and the crossing time was 2 hours 45 minutes. Sleeping carriages were provided on night trains to and from Paddington, though they were probably not much used in the outward direction; leaving London at 8.45pm, the occupant of a sleeping berth would have had to turn out at Fishguard at the inhospitable hour of 2.15am!

The GWR bought three express turbine steamers to operate the new service, *St George, St David* and *St Patrick*; the first was built by Cammell Laird, the others by John Brown at Clydebank. They were virtually sister ships, although *St George* was slightly longer. Accommodation was for 1,000 passengers, 562 in 1st Class and 438 in 3rd. There were 47 two- or four-berth cabins in 1st Class,

Pembroke aground on Little Saltees island. *Courtesy of National Library of Ireland*

located on the promenade, main and lower decks. The 1st Class dining saloon was on the main deck and in it 75 passengers could dine at detached tables, rather than the long tables of most contemporary ships. On the promenade deck the novel feature of a large lounge forward, referred to as a drawing room, allowed passengers to sit in comfort in 'alcoves and cosy corners', while there was an oak-panelled smoke room amidships. Steerage passengers had a dining saloon and ladies' cabin on the main deck aft and open-berth sleeping rooms on the main and lower decks. As the service initially seemed to be doing well, it was decided that a fourth ship was needed, and in 1908 *St Andrew* was built by John Brown.

A fine view of *St Patrick.* *Author's collection*

St David as a hospital ship during the First World War. *Author's collection*

When contraction set in on the cross-channel service, *St George* was sold in 1913 to the Canadian Pacific Railway for service across the Bay of Fundy. Her stay in Canada was short and in 1915 she was back in Britain as a hospital ship. After the war she was sold to the Great Eastern Railway for the Harwich-Hoek service, and broken up in 1929. *Author's collection*

In Ireland the Great Southern & Western Railway built a fine set of coaches for the Rosslare-Cork boat train, by means of which passengers could arrive in Cork at 9.20pm or 09.20am, and Killarney at 10.10pm or 10.35am. This represented a very considerable acceleration over the connections via Dublin. One of these carriages has fortunately been preserved by the Railway Preservation Society of Ireland. Trips to Killarney were offered, leaving Paddington on Friday evening and returning on Sunday morning, but it is not recorded how many people actually had the stamina for such a marathon, involving two changes at Fishguard in the small hours!

Even greater things were planned for Fishguard by the GWR, which hoped to develop a transatlantic port. In 1909 this seemed to be

St Andrew of 1932 alongside at Fishguard in June 1965. *Author*

Above An evening scene at Rosslare harbour on 18 June 1965, with *St Andrew* on the right and *St David* beyond. *Author*

Below *St David* outward bound in Fishguard Bay in June 1965. *Author*

happening, when Cunard Line began to call to land express mail that had formerly been unloaded at Queenstown and sent on via Holyhead. In 1910 14,000 passengers and 55,000 mail bags were landed. However, Cunard soon followed its rival the White Star Line to Southampton and Fishguard saw no more liners. It may also be questioned if the new facilities ever really repaid their cost, let alone earned more for the company. From 1908 the Rosslare service was worked by four ships, on the pattern of the Holyhead mail service, but as early as 1913 this was reduced to three and subsequently to two, providing only one sailing per day in each direction. By the 1950s the winter service had been reduced to three sailings per week in each direction. It was only the beginning of a car ferry service in 1965 that ensured the long-term survival of Fishguard as a cross-channel port, and it has thrived since then. However, an attempt to provide a service to Dun Laoghaire in the summer of 1978 failed to attract much traffic and was not repeated in following years.

Right An information pack for the associated car-carrier train that for some years ran from London to Fishguard and helped to increase the popularity of the service. *Author's collection*

Above and below A deck view aboard *Lord Warden* on 30 August 1978, while working the service to Dun Laoghaire, and the ship at Fishguard. As can be seen, this service attracted few passengers. *Author*

15. WATERFORD AND ITS SHIPS

The excellent natural harbour formed by the River Suir has long made Waterford a focal point in the traffic between Britain and Ireland. Various English kings passed through it (usually with a large army) and Queen Victoria used it as an overnight anchorage when en route form Cork

Dunbrody **loads at Waterford amid scenes of ordered chaos! She was built at Glasgow in 1886, to the characteristic old-fashioned design favoured by the Waterford Company, with funnel aft, but her refrigerated holds, lit by electricity, were thoroughly up-to-date. In one of her single-berth cabins there was a bed of extra width to suit the needs of a regular passenger who, like the ship herself, was built for comfort rather than speed! As the CSC's** *Arklow* **she remained in service until 1931.** *Courtesy of National Museums Liverpool, Merseyside Maritime Museum*

to Dublin in August 1849, but did not bother to land to see the city.

As early as 1826 Waterford had acquired its own steam shipping company, the Waterford & Bristol SS Company, whose title gradually became abbreviated to the Waterford SS Co. In the mid-19th century it ran deep-sea as well as cross-channel ships. The driving force behind this enterprise was William Malcolmson, who was also chairman of what was then the Waterford & Limerick Railway, as well as running the Neptune iron foundry in the city and an associated shipyard. The company also operated tugs, and in 1884 had two, *Rossa* and *Dauntless*, as well as river steamers *Tintern* (1861) and *Ida* (1868) on the

Suir; both of these had been built in the Waterford yard. As mentioned elsewhere, it also ran steamers on the Shannon. However, by 1900 this heyday had passed and the river services came to an end with the opening of railway lines to Rosslare and New Ross early in the 20th century. Thereafter the Waterford company confined itself to serving Bristol and Liverpool. In 1912 it sold out for £54,000 to the Clyde Shipping Company, whose vessels had long served the port from Glasgow. To this company were transferred three ships – the elderly *Reginald* and *Dunbrody* and the relatively new *Clodagh* of 1904 – and the purchase also gave the CSC entry to Liverpool and Bristol. The

Above Slightly further downstream but amid the same conditions, the Clyde Shipping Company's *Eddystone* and another of its ships are loading. The former was built at Dundee in 1886 and sold by the company in 1923 for service in Greece, where she lasted until sunk by a bomb in 1941. She was then salvaged and taken to Italy and is thought to have been finally scrapped in 1946, after quite a fine career. The quayside operation seems to have been very labour-intensive, but just beside the little hut on the right is a group of four men who have clearly come along to watch the action and enjoy a bit of a crack. *Courtesy of National Library of Ireland*

Below A view of *Reginald* at sea. She was built on the Clyde in 1878 and sold to the Admiralty in 1914, to serve as a block ship at Scapa Flow. *Courtesy of National Museums Liverpool, Merseyside Maritime Museum*

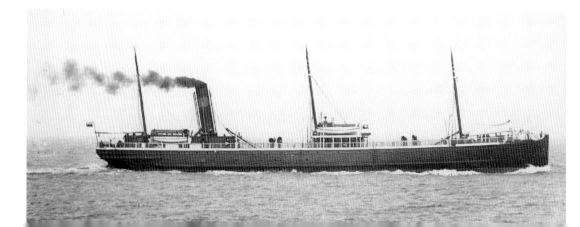

Above The Clyde Shipping Company's *Ballycotton* on the Clyde off Gourock. With her sister *Warner* she had her passenger accommodation amidships, an innovation for the CSC. She was sold to Palgrave, Murphy & Co of Dublin in 1936 and, despite being a neutral ship, was torpedoed in 1940. *Glasgow University Archives*

Below *Toward* of the Clyde Shipping Company (1923) in the River Suir. She was lost in 1943 while serving as a convoy rescue ship. *Courtesy of National Library of Ireland*

Bottom *Clodagh* on the River Suir in the Waterford Company's colours. *Courtesy of National Library of Ireland*

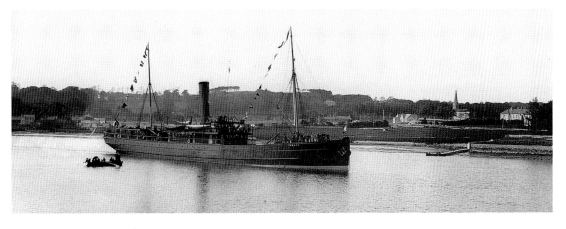

Waterford crews were retained but captains and officers now came from Scotland.

The new owners did not use the first of the three, but kept the others, renaming them *Arklow* and *Coningbeg* respectively. The latter was used on the Liverpool service, now partnered by the CSC's own new *Formby*, built, unusually for a CSC ship, at Dundee in 1914. *Coningbeg* was also thoroughly rebuilt and, according to company publicity, 'electrified', which presumably referred to the lighting. She was now typical of the CSC fleet, having accommodation for 86 in 1st Class and 74 in steerage. The dining saloon for the former could seat 27, at three tables for nine, and there was also a small smoke room. A high standard of catering was offered, as shown by a menu from *Formby* dated 30 July 1914:

Salmon Mayonnaise
Roast beef   Roast lamb   Pressed beef
Ham and tongue
Swiss tart   Jellies   Compot of fruit
Cheese   Salad
Coffee

There were three sailings per week in each direction between Waterford and Liverpool, the passage taking about 15 hours. Fares in cabin were 17s 6d single and 23 shillings return, but a four-day return was available for 20 shillings. Steerage fares were 10 and 15 shillings. Through bookings were available to a wide range of railway stations in England. There was also an attractive range of tours from Waterford. One could have an eight-day trip to London, calling at Southampton, Newhaven and Dover on the outward journey and Plymouth on the return, for £1 10s 0d, exclusive of meals. This facility was useful to those who might feel unwell in the Channel, or who wanted to eat ashore at a port of call. Tours to Glasgow via either Liverpool or Dublin were also offered, in conjunction with both G. & J. Burns and Laird Line. It was a civilised way of travelling.

By late 1917, with Britain in the grip of the German submarine blockade, matters had become much less civilised and the Waterford route had assumed great importance in the food supply chain that was only just keeping the country going. In December of that year totals of 2,914 cattle, 927 sheep and 1,079 pigs were shipped to England

through Waterford. The Germans were no doubt aware of the importance of the route, and their submarines were now prowling in the Irish Sea. In December 1917 U62 left her base at Heligoland, under the command of Commander Ernst Hashagen. He was a professional sailor, intent on doing his duty to Kaiser and country, but he was not a monster and in earlier days, when the war was conducted in a more gentlemanly fashion, always took care that survivors of an attack were safe before he left them.

In due course U62 tucked herself into Caernarfon Bay to observe the shipping scene and allow Hashagen to assess how and where he could inflict maximum damage. Unlike his colleague in 1918, he did not fancy his chances with the Irish Mail steamers – 'big two-chimneyed steamers', as he noted on 15 December. They were fast, often adopted a zig-zag course and on one occasion one was accompanied by a destroyer. But elsewhere, as he observed, 'There is plenty of scope for attack.' He started with the Dublin & Manchester Company's *Hare*, which sank with the loss of 15 lives. On the evening of 15 December he caught up with *Formby* en route from Liverpool, off Anglesey at 7.58pm, and fired a torpedo that penetrated the engine room. She sank immediately with the loss of all 39 on board, only the body of the stewardess ever being found.

That night and during the morning of Sunday the 16th, a fierce storm raged over the south-east of Ireland, bringing down telephone wires and effectively cutting off Waterford from the outside world. Initially there was not too much alarm when *Formby* did not appear as scheduled, since it seemed likely that she had taken shelter from the storm and would turn up in due course. Therefore no warning was sent out to alert other ships of the presence of U62, and in the late afternoon of Monday the 17th *Coningbeg* set out from Liverpool for her home port, having on board a crew of 40 and four passengers, almost all being from the Waterford area. Again U62 found her off Anglesey, but she was travelling at speed, the storm having abated, and, totally unaware that he was being stalked, Captain J. Lumley in fact gave the submarine a hard chase. It was not until about midnight, after 4 hours of pursuit, that Hashagen decided that the time was ripe to attack and two torpedoes were fired. Two explosions broke the

The memorial stones on the river front at Waterford to those who lost their lives on board *Formby* and *Coningbeg* in 1917. *Author*

Coningbeg's back and she went down immediately with no survivors. Having watched with a sense of awe and having checked that there were no survivors, Hashagen made off and for some days remained in the area to wreak further havoc, before returning to base on Christmas Eve to enjoy some holiday leave.

It was a miserable Christmas in Waterford. Day after day, in wet snow, wives and mothers went to the shipping office to try to get some news, but it

was not until 27 December that the Clyde Company wrote to family members to say that the ships must be assumed to have been lost. A disaster fund was set up to help dependants and in due course raised almost £8,000. It was certainly needed – the family of fireman J. Wall, one of ten employed on *Coningbeg*, were no doubt grateful for any help offered, as his widow was left with seven young children to maintain.

These two ordinary little ships, going about their everyday business, made no headlines in their lives nor in their deaths; by 1917 the world was only too used to such happenings to pay much attention. But their loss was a cruel blow to the city where they belonged, and the appeals to the disaster fund continued for many years. Today the memorials by the river keep their story alive.

Great Western of 1902 was built at Birkenhead for the GWR and initially ran from New Milford, transferring to Fishguard in 1906. Much of her later time was spent on the Waterford route, although she also sailed from Weymouth to the Channel Islands, and this photograph shows her in Weymouth Bay. She was withdrawn in 1933. *Author's collection*

Great Western of 1934. *World Ship Society*

There were of course other services from Waterford, including that to Glasgow maintained by the Clyde Shipping Company in its own right, but the main one for passenger traffic was that to various ports in West Wales, maintained in one way or another from 1824 to 1959. From 1872 this service was maintained by the Great Western Railway, and in 1906 the eastern terminal was transferred to Fishguard. From 1934 this service was maintained by a single ship, which bore the name of her owners, *Great Western*. Her looks have been criticised by other authors, but she was reliable and a good sea boat, and until the 1950s attracted a loyal clientele. She sailed on three nights a week from each port, dovetailing with the service to Cork. The westbound schedule was a comfortable one – in 1954 a train left London

Paddington at 3.45pm and the ship sailed from Fishguard at midnight, allowing passengers to enjoy breakfast next morning during the pleasant sail up the Suir. In the reverse direction departure was at 6.30pm, but this involved a change at Fishguard at the ungodly hour of 2.00am, with almost 2 hours to wait until the London train left. If they so wished, passengers could remain on board until 7.00am, but of course this considerably lengthened the overall journey time.

For those in 1st Class *Great Western* provided two-berth cabins, but in steerage there were only open berths; charges for these were 7 and 3 shillings respectively. Cars were conveyed, at rates that started at £7 7s 1d for those under 10cwt, about £200 at present-day values. Numbers declined from about 1956 and the passenger service came to an end in 1959. Adelphi Wharf, from which the ship sailed, has been converted into luxury apartments.

16. SOME SMALLER PORTS

Sligo

This port had been a centre of a thriving passenger trade in the early days of steamships, many of those passing through it being emigrants fleeing famine in Ireland, and some of the ships sailing from it became notorious for the treatment of steerage passengers. However, with the coming of the railway to the west of Ireland, this traffic declined, since all but the very poorest could now get to Derry or Belfast in relative comfort and so avoid what was often a stormy passage around Donegal. Services then settled down to cater mainly for cattle and cargo, with a few passengers being carried; in later years these were mostly round-trip holidaymakers. The harbour at Sligo had a rail connection to the Midland & Great Western Railway and this greatly facilitated the cattle traffic. When a new ship entered service in 1864, local commentators enthused about the covered accommodation for livestock on board, no mention being made of any shelter for steerage passengers, which showed where the priorities lay!

The Sligo Steam Navigation Company was set up in 1857 by two local businessmen to serve both Glasgow and Liverpool. However, they soon made an agreement with Laird Line to serve the former, and concentrated on Liverpool only. This they did until August 1936, when they became part of Burns Laird Lines. The two Sligo services were then amalgamated and served by one ship on a weekly basis; they came to an end in 1954.

The Sligo company did not carry passengers after 1914, but Laird, and later Burns Laird, revived this traffic in 1920 and it continued until 1936. Latterly the Sligo company owned successive ships named after the town; that of 1889 ran aground just outside the harbour in a snowstorm in 1912 when carrying a load of coal. The crew remained on board until the next day, when they climbed down on to the beach and reached the town dryshod, but the ship herself was a total loss. She was replaced by another ship of the same name, which was sold to Limerick owners in 1918 and was in turn replaced by the City of Dublin SP company's *Carrickfergus*, which lasted until 1929. A new *Sligo* was then built in 1930, by the Dublin Dockyard Company.

In pre-1914 days the Laird Line ships sailed from Glasgow on Wednesdays and Saturdays, at 2.00pm and 12 noon respectively, the Saturday sailing continuing alternately to Ballina and Westport.

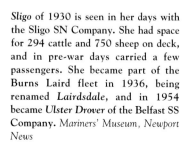

Sligo of 1930 is seen in her days with the Sligo SN Company. She had space for 294 cattle and 750 sheep on deck, and in pre-war days carried a few passengers. She became part of the Burns Laird fleet in 1936, being renamed *Lairdsdale*, and in 1954 became *Ulster Drover* of the Belfast SS Company. *Mariners' Museum, Newport News*

Fares to any of those destinations were 12s 6d single, 20 shillings return in cabin, and 5 and 8 shillings in steerage. Local passengers were also carried between Sligo and Ballina or Westport.

For some, the danger began with the trip to connect with the Glasgow steamer. On 14 June 1894 a group of harvesters sailed from Achill in a hooker – a local sailing boat – for Westport, where they would connect with Laird's *Gardenia* for Glasgow. While they were crossing Clew Bay a summer storm passed over and the vessel capsized, drowning all 32 on board. The bodies of the harvesters were taken back to Achill on the newly constructed but not yet opened railway line.

Below Lairdsbank (the former *Olive*) at Ballina. A typical workhorse of the Irish Sea, she was built by D. & W. Henderson in May 1893. Despite sailing on one of the most exposed routes around the coasts of the British Isles, her only serious accident came, not when she was battling a storm off Aranmore, but when she was snugly tied up in Sligo harbour on the night of 27 February 1902, when carrying a load of Indian corn from Glasgow. A gale arose and she was blown right across the harbour and on to the opposite shore. Although she was not seriously damaged, she was so high and dry that she could not be refloated until a powerful tug arrived from Glasgow to free her. None the worse of this adventure, she lasted with Burns Laird until 1930, then had seven years of service to the Orkneys with the North of Scotland company. *G. E. Langmuir collection, the Mitchell Library, Glasgow City Council*

Below The same ship on trials on the measured mile at Skelmorlie on the Clyde. The white posts that marked the start and finish of the mile can be seen on the shore to the left. *Glasgow University Archives*

2740

GLASGOW BOAT AT COLERAINE.

Coleraine

Although steamers ran from this small port in the 1860s, it was not until 1884 that regular services began, following the deepening of the channel at the bar at the mouth of the River Bann. Laird Line operated a twice-weekly service for many years, but by 1905 this had been reduced to one trip per week. This left Glasgow on Monday at midday and passengers could join the ship at Greenock via a train leaving at 4.35pm. Fares in that year were 10 shillings single, 14 shillings return in 1st Class and only 2s 6d in steerage, just over half the fare to Derry. By 1912 these had increased to 11 shillings and 16s 6d in 1st and 4s 6d single in steerage. The timetable stated 'with liberty to call at Ballycastle and Portrush', but it is not clear how often such calls were actually made. Normally some of the smaller ships of this line were used, none of which provided any accommodation for steerage passengers; these had to remain on deck or take their chance among the animals and merchandise in the forward cargo space. For cabin passengers on ships such as *Olive* there was a dining saloon aft on the main deck, with cabins opening from it, and there were also berths at the after end of the saloon itself. The service ended with the outbreak of war in 1914.

Lily approaches Coleraine on the River Bann. She was built for the Laird Line in 1896 and was used mainly on the Portrush service until the appearance of *Hazel* in 1907. She thereafter served Coleraine for a few years until transferred to give excursions out of Ayr during the Glasgow Fair holidays in 1913 and 1914, in opposition to the G&SWR paddler *Juno*, which would seem to have been a somewhat unequal contest! After the war she ran mainly to Sligo and in 1929 became *Lairdspool*. From 1936 she was chartered to David MacBrayne Ltd and became *Lochgorm*. She ran from Glasgow to Stornoway until 1951, when she was scrapped after an unspectacular but successful career typical of many of the smaller Irish Sea ships of the time. Details of her accommodation have not survived, but it is likely that the dining saloon was on the main deck aft, surrounded by cabins. *Author's collection*

Silloth and the Solway

Having reached Carlisle by the 'Waverley Route' from Edinburgh in 1862, the North British Railway, which was then pursuing an aggressively expansionist policy, immediately leased the railway lines to Silloth and Port Carlisle and, by an Act of the following year, gained powers to operate steamers from either of these places to Belfast. A fine paddle steamer, *Waverley*, was put on the service in 1864 and was succeeded by a slightly larger ship of the same name the following

Left In the 1890s the service from Silloth to Liverpool was profitable and it was decided to buy a new ship to replace the elderly *Silloth*. *Kittiwake* came from the Bowling yard of Scott & Co in 1896 and ran from Silloth until April 1919. She seems normally to have carried about 12-15 passengers per voyage in pre-1914 days, when ships left Silloth 'on most days' on one high tide and arrived in the Mersey in time for the next. Cabin fares were 7 shillings single and 10s 6d return, and the steerage fare was 8s 6d return. When the service ceased she was sold to the Dundalk & Newry SP Company and sailed for them until 1929. The other ship still on the route in 1919, *Albatross* of 1878, was sold to Turkish owners and ran between Constantinople/Istanbul and Izmir as *Tayyar*. Incredibly she was in service, albeit much rebuilt and dieselised, until 1994, and was still afloat at Tuzla in 2002. She may well still be there! This view shows *Kittiwake* arriving at Silloth. *C. Puxley collection*

Left To cope with all the shipping using Silloth in the 1890s, the NBR company bought this attractive little tug, *Solway*, in 1886; she was sold to Grimsby owners in 1917. It would seem from this photograph that she carried out excursions in addition to her normal duties. *C. Puxley collection*

Below Trade obviously expanded to the point where one tug could not always cope on her own, and in 1897 a second, *Petrel*, was built by Renoldson of South Shields and lasted into the days of British Railways. In this view she is towing a barque into the harbour. The pier in the background, long a favourite promenade of holidaymakers, later succumbed to the shifting sands of the Solway and no longer exists. *Author's collection*

Homeward Bound Entering, Silloth Docks

year. However, the company hit a financial crisis in 1866 and she was sold in 1868. Thereafter the railway company confined its own sailings to a passenger and cargo service from Silloth to Liverpool, which ran until 1919. The NBR took steps to develop the port and, after the existing dock had been damaged by an inrush of water, opened a new one in 1885. It was from this dock that the company's own ships sailed, although trade at Silloth was by no means confined to these; many other ships called, in particular those bringing grain to the flour mills.

From 1869 to 1892, a service was run from Silloth to Douglas and Dublin by the North British Silloth Steam Packet Company, but in the latter year this became a joint venture with William Sloan & Co, whose usual route was from Glasgow to the Bristol Channel. For it a new ship was built and, following Sloan's usual practice of naming its ships after rivers, she became *Yarrow*. Through bookings were available from NBR stations, and publicity stressed that it was possible to go by this route from Edinburgh to Dublin via the Scott country. It was, however, a fair and

A postcard view of *Yarrow* arriving at Silloth. *Author's collection*

totally unsheltered walk from the railway station to the ship's berth.

Yarrow had fairly extensive passenger accommodation, with a saloon and two-berth cabins. In addition she had stalls for 500 cattle and pens for 200 sheep or pigs, together with holds for 150 tons of general cargo. Inbound from Ireland, Guinness formed a large part of the cargo. She seems to have been quite well patronised, although someone later commented that she had seldom been overcrowded, and when she ran on to a sandbank near Silloth in 1919 – her only adventure - she was carrying between 60 and 70 people. The writer of a postcard of around 1914 mentioned that the family had gone down to see her arrive on an occasion when she carried 53 passengers, 212 cows and 56 pigs. Apparently 'baby loved it'. Her crew members remained with her for many years. In 1921 she was commanded by Captain William Kearney of Dublin and the two stewards were Billy Adams and Paddy Byrne, while Miss Scott served as stewardess. Mr Byrne lived in Silloth until the early 1980s.

In 1929 *Yarrow* was in need of a refit and questions were being asked by the Board of Trade about the state of her boilers. The estimated cost of refitting and reboilering her was £5,000, a sum

Yarrow entering Silloth Harbour

that the NBR's successor, the LNER, clearly could not afford. She was therefore transferred to Irish registry, being sold to the Dublin & Silloth SS Company, managed by Palgrave, Murphy & Co of Dublin, which later took her over, although a close connection with the LNER was maintained. She was renamed *Assaroe* and given the Palgrave, Murphy funnel colouring of yellow with a green band and black top. Single-berth cabins were now available, at an extra charge of 5 shillings per journey, and she boasted a 'wireless'. The passenger service ended with the outbreak of war and all sailings ceased in 1943. *Assaroe* then sailed between Ireland and Spain, mainly with horses, and was broken up in Belgium in 1947.

At the other end there were cheap weekend tickets to Galway and Sligo via the M&GWR and to Killarney via the G&SWR, as well as 'attractive tours' at low fares (not specified) to Killarney and Connemara. Sailings were twice weekly in each direction, and in 1929 these left Silloth on Tuesdays and Saturdays and Dublin on Mondays and Thursdays, the actual time being dependent on the tides at Silloth. An example for 2 July 1910 shows a connecting train from Glasgow at 1.00pm and from Edinburgh at 2.00pm, with a departure at 6.30pm from Silloth to give an arrival in Douglas at 12.30am and in Dublin early the following morning. The times at Douglas were not always convenient – the return working of that given above left the Manx town at 3.00am, allowing passengers to reach Glasgow at about 4.00pm. A single passage to either port then cost 10 shillings saloon and 5 shillings

In these views, taken in 1935, *Yarrow* is seen arriving at Silloth and landing her passengers at the entrance to the New Dock, before making her way to her own berth. *Both C. Puxley collection*

Countess of Galloway leaving Garlieston for Liverpool.
Author's collection

steerage, which had risen by 1929 to 12s 6d and 8 shillings to Douglas and 20 shillings and 12s 6d to Dublin. Returns were also available to the latter, at 30 and 20 shillings. Fares from Glasgow to either Douglas or Dublin in 1895 were 17s 6d and 29s 3d 1st Class and saloon, or 8s 8d and 14s 6d 3rd and steerage. These fares were competitive with Laird Line fares and of course offered a shorter sea passage, but it is debatable how many actually used this roundabout route.

The port of Silloth remains busy, but the ships that call now are larger than those that formerly sailed to and from Ireland and bring cargoes from much further afield.

The Silloth steamers were not the only ones to run out of the Solway. The small port of Garlieston in Wigtownshire, connected to the rail network by the cash-strapped Wigtownshire Railway, was used by coastal steamers from the mid-1830s onwards, one of the best known being *Countess of Galloway*, a paddle steamer built in 1835 for service to Liverpool; she lived on until 1880, by which time she had become something a local institution. That service ended in 1875, but the old girl still had some life left in her and continued to sail between Stranraer and Liverpool until 1879. Latterly those ships that called were mainly on excursion trips to the Isle of Man or, occasionally, Blackpool. Mostly these trips were

undertaken by IOMSP steamers, but occasionally those of Laird Line also called, as on 6 August 1888, when *Elm* operated a trip leaving Garlieston at 8.30am, arriving in Douglas at midday and giving passengers more than 5 hours ashore, before bringing them home by 9.15pm; fares were 4 shillings or 2s 6d. The last such trip was taken by the IOM Company's *Victoria* in 1953, but in recent years *Balmoral* has revived this cruise, which has been so successful that it is now given on an annual basis.

Dundalk and Newry

The Dundalk & Newry Steam Packet Co was formed in 1871 by a merger of the Dundalk SP Co, which dated back to 1837, and the Newry SP Co, which was a relative junior, being only three years old at he time of the merger. There was a close association with the Dundalk & Enniskillen Railway that continued after the latter was absorbed into the GNR(I) in 1876. The main service was from both Dundalk and Newry to Liverpool, but sailings to Ardrossan and Glasgow were operated until just before the First World War. The superior facilities of the Greenore route attracted traffic away from Dundalk and Newry after 1873 and passenger services ceased in 1918. The partition of Ireland led to a further decline in the use of the route and the company was taken over by the British & Irish Steam Packet Co in 1928.

Above The remarkable *Earl of Erne* was built at Port Glasgow in 1855 and carried passengers and cargo from Dundalk to Liverpool until June 1918, by which time she was the last paddle steamer sailing between Britain and Ireland. There was accommodation for 40 saloon passengers and a dormitory for drovers, cattle always being an important source of revenue for the Dundalk company. In 1888 she received a new compound engine and, despite being one of the slowest ships on the Irish Sea during the First World War, she managed to avoid the attentions of the U-boat commanders. Even in 1918 she was not finished and was sold to Greek owners, who sailed her until she was wrecked in 1926. In this view she seems to be on an excursion trip of some kind – she was not normally so crowded! *Courtesy of National Museums Liverpool, Merseyside Maritime Museum*

Below The rather neat little steamer *Bessbrook* was built for the Dundalk & Newry Co by A. & J. Inglis of Glasgow in 1877 and was still with the company when sold to the B&I company in 1928. Initially she sailed mainly to Ardrossan, but latterly to Liverpool. *Andrew McQueen, Glasgow University Archives*

Above A lady passenger, probably Miss McQueen, on board *Bessbrook*. *Andrew McQueen, Glasgow University Archives*

Below The cargo steamer *Vigilant* of 1884 on the Newry Canal. She was built for Messrs Bacon, a company that later became Powell, Bacon & Hough and, later still, in 1913, became a part of the Coast Lines group. *Glasgow University Archives*

Above A view of Ramsden Dock, with *Duchess of Devonshire* on the right and, behind her, *Duchess of Buccleuch*, with a dredger on the left. Both passenger ships are wearing Barrow SN Company colours. *Duchess of Devonshire* was one of those little ships that led an unspectacular but thoroughly useful career. She was built in Barrow in 1897 by what was then the naval Construction & Armament Company, as a dual-purpose to serve Douglas in summer and, with some additional cabins, Belfast in winter. The Midland Railway kept her on the former service and she lasted with its successor, the LMS, until 1928, when she was sold to Messrs Bland of Gibraltar. She sailed from the colony to Tangier until 1940, and was then used as an accommodation ship until 1944. She was finally scrapped in 1949. *Duchess of Buccleuch*, a paddle steamer, had been built as *Rouen* for the London, Brighton & South Coast Railway in 1888 and came to Barrow in 1903. She was used on the Douglas service until broken up in 1909. *McLean Museum & Art Gallery, Inverclyde Council*

Below *Duchess of Buccleuch* is leaving Morecambe for Douglas. Morecambe had been a cross-channel port before Heysham was opened, but this looks like an excursion sailing, the town having developed more as a holiday resort by the early 20th century. *M. Walker, Lancaster City Museum*

Barrow

In terms of cross-channel traffic, Barrow has always played a minor role. This was not due to a lack of facilities at the port, which were always quite good and, from the opening of Ramsden Dock station in 1881, became really first class, since trains now ran alongside the steamers and passengers could transfer under cover. Barrow's drawback was its geographical location.

In 1877 a guide book mentioned the new route from Dublin to England via Barrow, which would operate after 6 April. Timings were not given, but the service would leave Barrow on Mondays and Thursdays and Dublin on Tuesdays and Fridays. To almost any English city or to Glasgow this must have been a very roundabout route, and one wonders how much traffic it actually carried. Steamers also ran to Belfast, Newry and (in summer) to Douglas; there were also services for Morecambe. These services were operated by the Barrow Steam Navigation Company, a joint venture of the Midland Railway, the Furness Railway and James Little & Co, begun in 1867. The Midland provided trains in connection, but passengers for overnight sailings had to leave St Pancras at 1.30pm, and on the return journey did not reach London until 3.30pm. The Dublin service clearly did not last long, but those to Belfast and Douglas continued even after the opening of Heysham in 1904, though the former was now only on three nights per week in each direction. In 1907 the four remaining Barrow SN Company ships became part of the Midland fleet, one being scrapped immediately. Services from Barrow ended with the First World War, and Ramsden Dock station finally closed in 1936. Since then the only sailings to operate out of Barrow have been occasional charter cruises by Isle of Man steamers.

Drogheda

Local initiative brought the benefits of steamship services to Drogheda at the fairly early date of 1826, when the Drogheda Steam Packet Company was founded to operate to Liverpool. The cattle trade was the mainstay of the company, the beasts simply being walked from the farms of Meath to the quays along the River Boyne. Due to the height at which the main Dublin-Belfast railway line crossed the river on the famous viaduct, the quays were not at any time connected to the rail network, but this does not seem to have affected the initial profitability of the DSPC in any way. Steerage passenger traffic was heavy in the early years, especially during and just after the famine of the 1840s when there was a daily service, but it then declined as the Irish rail network developed and migrants found it easier to take a train to Dublin and go by ship from there. The service by the 1870s had come down to four sailings a week in each direction, fares being 10 shillings saloon and 4 shillings steerage.

The company catered well for the local market and saw no need to venture further afield, apart from providing infrequent sailings to Glasgow, but by the late 1890s it was in difficulties and, under a new manager who had come from the LNWR at North Wall, began to discuss a take-over by the Lancashire & Yorkshire Railway. This alarmed the City of Dublin Company, who petitioned Parliament against the merger, but this only served to delay it and in May 1902 the L&YR acquired the DSPC. It then made efforts to develop the traffic, particularly by encouraging 1st Class passengers, but these were unsuccessful and it probably lost a good deal of money on this venture. Passenger services ended in 1914. In 1928 the LMS was no doubt glad to be able to transfer the cargo service to the British & Irish Steam Packet Co.

The Drogheda Company was unusual among Irish Sea operators in that it did not at any time operate a screw-propelled ship, relying on paddle steamers to the end. However, this should not be taken to imply that it was old-fashioned, as it introduced such features as compound and, later, triple- and quadruple-expansion engines long before such giants as the LNWR did; the *Colleen Bawn* of 1862 introduced the former to the Irish Sea, while *Iverna* of 1895 pioneered the latter. It simply seems to have been a case of knowing best which type could provide the service required by the local traders and passengers in the most economical way. The fares quoted above were not changed from 1849 until almost 60 years later.

The L&YR clearly did not think much of the fleet it acquired in 1902 and immediately placed an order with Vickers of Barrow for two modern screw ships.

Above A painting of *Tredach* of 1876. She introduced the novelty of steam-operated machinery for working the winches, and also steam steering gear. More than 50 passengers could be accommodated in 1st Class berths, and the accommodation was noted as being very comfortable. She was withdrawn when the new railway steamers appeared in 1903. *Old Drogheda Society*

Below A photograph of the same ship on the Clyde. *Glasgow University Archives*

Packed to the gunnels with local passengers enjoying a church outing, *Nora Creina* of 1878 steams down the Boyne – the railway viaduct can just be discerned in the background. This ship was almost a sister to *Tredach*, but lasted until 1912. *Old Drogheda Society*

Above The last ship to be acquired by the Drogheda SP Company, and the last paddle steamer to be built for service between Britain and Ireland, was *Iverna,* built by A. & J. Inglis at Glasgow in 1895; her name is thought to be a form of 'Hibernia'. Although she looked very old-fashioned, with a single funnel aft of the paddles, she was really quite up-to-date, with quadruple-expansion machinery and steam heating. Accommodation for about 500 cattle was provided in well-ventilated quarters. The L&YR retained her on the service until 1912, when she was sold for scrapping. She is seen here in dock at Liverpool. *Courtesy of National Museums Liverpool, Merseyside Maritime Museum*

Below The same ship on trials on the Clyde. *Glasgow University Archives*

These appeared in 1903 and were named *Colleen Bawn* and *Mellifont*. Excellent accommodation was provided for saloon passengers, who now travelled amidships instead of in the stern, as on the paddlers. The dining saloon was located on the promenade deck, and also had berths for 22. There were five four-berth cabins, a ladies' cabin with 12 berths, and a smoke room, which could also provide eight berths. Separate rooms for male and female steerage passengers were provided on the main deck aft, and there was also a bar.

However, despite the new ships, through fares to many stations in England, and free transfer from train to ship in Liverpool, the service did not prosper and as early as 1906 *Mellifont* was transferred to the railway's East Coast services, returning to Drogheda in 1912 when the last paddle steamer, *Iverna* of 1895, was withdrawn. Both ships remained on the Drogheda route until the railway company disposed of it in 1928, after which they sailed on relief services from Holyhead until withdrawal in 1931 and 1933 respectively.

Above **Mellifont** in dock at Holyhead in LMS days. *Courtesy of National Museums Liverpool, Merseyside Maritime Museum*

Below One of the L&YR ships, in original colours, on the Boyne. The photograph has been altered to enclose the after end of the midships section. *Author's collection*

Drogheda and Liverpool Steamer on the Boyne.

17. IRISH COASTAL AND INLAND SERVICES

Galway Bay

One of the first acts of the Congested Districts Board (see below under 'The Shannon') was to start a regular steamer service connecting Galway with the three Aran Islands. This it arranged by paying a subsidy to the Galway Bay Steamboat Company, which placed its paddle tug *Citie of the Tribes* on the service. However, a purpose-built screw steamer, *Duras*, was built in the following year and lasted until 1912, when she was replaced by the larger *Dun Aengus*, which in 1951 was taken over by CIE. She gave excellent service until 1958, when the motorship *Naomh Eanna* was built in Dublin. She brought vastly superior

passenger accommodation and also had a sick-bay on board, for patients travelling from the islands to hospital in Galway. In 1964 she was joined by a newcomer.

Galway Bay had begun life in 1930 as *Calshot* with the Red Funnel line at Southampton, as a tender to ocean liners in the Solent. In 1964 the Holland-Amerika Line instituted calls by its ocean liners at Galway and acquired this ship to act as tender and also to provide excursions when not so occupied. She was refitted at a cost of £100,000 and was certainly a well-appointed little ship, although her considerable beam made her more

Galway Bay laid up at Penzance in April 1969. *Author*

prone to rolling in more exposed waters than many of her passengers appreciated. On most days she left Galway in the morning, cruised around the Aran Islands and called at Kilronan on Inishmore, the largest island, before returning to Galway in the evening. Actual sailing times varied according to the tide, while return fares varied according to the day of the week, between 24 and 30 shillings. A few sailings were also given from Ballyvaughan. She seemed to be quite successful, but when Holland-Amerika withdrew the Galway calls in 1968, she too was withdrawn. She is now preserved at Southampton, although recently her future has been in doubt.

Below Naomh Eanna leaves Galway. In the summer of 1965 she generally sailed on four days per week – Tuesday, Thursday, Saturday and Sunday – on some days doing a round of the islands, while on others making a simple out-and-back trip to Kilronan on Inishmore, the only point to have a pier. At the other islands passengers and goods were ferried ashore in curraghs. Departure times from Galway varied between 7.00am and midday, and she generally arrived back about 5.00-6.00pm. The complete round of the islands, which seems to have operated in the summer months only, took between 9 and 11 hours, which gave the possibility of a day ashore on Inishmore. In July, due to the amount of passenger traffic, livestock was carried only on fair days, the 19th and the 22nd. *Author's collection*

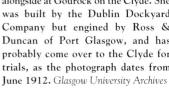

Below left   Dun Aengus coming alongside at Gourock on the Clyde. She was built by the Dublin Dockyard Company but engined by Ross & Duncan of Port Glasgow, and has probably come over to the Clyde for trials, as the photograph dates from June 1912. Glasgow University Archives

Below   Publicity for Galway Bay's sailings. Author's collection

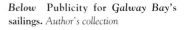

Day Trips and Charters
PORT AND LINER SERVICES (IRELAND) LTD.

"NESS QUEEN" AT BRIDGE-CAPPOQUIN.

The Blackwater

The River Blackwater in the south-east of Ireland has sometimes been called 'the Irish Rhine', although it has to be said that a little imagination may be required when making the comparison. However, it is certainly a pleasant river and pleasure steamers operated on it at various times up to the First World War. Round trips were facilitated when the Cork & Youghal Railway reached the former coastal resort and village, and a steamer named *Daisy* was run in connection with trains for some years, sailing up to Cappoquin. However, she was essentially a tug, and was soon replaced by a vessel named *Fairy*, which lasted for about ten years on the river. The service then lapsed until revived in 1893 by a ship named *Sybil*, which was joined three years later by *Ness Queen*, a pretty little paddle steamer with a clipper bow and bowsprit. The cost of a cruise on board the latter was 1 shilling. She seems to have sailed until 1905, then there was a break until 1907 when a former River Dart steamer, *Dartmouth Castle*, was placed in service. A circular tour was offered for 6 shillings – train from Cork to Youghal, a 2-hour sail up the river on the steamer, and a return train ride from Cappoquin to Cork, changing at

Photographs of steamers on the Blackwater are rare and the inclusion of this rather poor view of *Ness Queen* at Cappoquin in the early 1900s may be justified on grounds of its rarity. The fine viaduct in the background carried the line of the Great Southern & Western Railway from Waterford to Cork via Fermoy. *Author's collection*

Mallow. The sailings came to an end in 1913 and no further attempt was made to carry passengers on the Blackwater.

Lough Erne

Steamers operated on Lough Erne from 1842 onwards, but for many years they carried both passengers and cargo, and anyone who took a cruise to see the charms of the lough had to be prepared to share the deck with a herd of cows. However, in 1868 a ship built for tourist traffic appeared, owned by one Mr H. D'Arch Irvine, who had a hotel at Rossclare, and the little steamer took her name from that place. Some time after his death, she was bought by a local syndicate, the Lough Erne Steamboat Company Ltd (in which the Sligo, Leitrim & Northern Counties Railway had an interest, perhaps a controlling interest), which persuaded the shipbuilding firm of Workman Clark in Belfast to

A postcard view of **Lady of the Lake** at Enniskillen. *Author's collection*

The Shannon

send a team of workmen to give her a very thorough overhaul. Re-named *Lady of the Lake*, she took up a regular service between Enniskillen and Castlecaldwell in 1896. At the latter place, connection was made with the trains of the Great Northern Railway to and from Bundoran, through fares being available. Picnic parties could be put off and collected at any of the many islands en route, and the *Lady* was very popular locally. There were also through bookings with the SL&NCR.

Sailings were suspended in 1914 and not resumed after the war, but the ship herself went on to have quite an exciting time during the troubles in the area in 1920/1. She had been acquired by a lady and converted to screw propulsion, for use as a motor yacht, but was requisitioned by the new administration of Northern Ireland to help quell disturbances at Belleek and Pettigo. She then reverted to her owner and was not finally scrapped until 1956.

Two screw steamers were also operated by a Mr J. G. Porter, who had a hotel at Knockninny. He ran them under the title of the 'Royal Erne Route', but the expected tourist traffic did not develop and both were used only for special charters until the owner died in 1903. More recently motor launches have offered local trips from Enniskillen.

Navigation on what is the longest river in the British Isles and the largest in Ireland has been carried on for centuries and was greatly facilitated by works carried out in the 18th and early 19th centuries. Around 1845 105,000 tons of merchandise and 20,000 passengers were carried on it annually. In the 1850s the Midland & Great Western Railway operated passenger steamers in an attempt to compete with the G&SWR for the Limerick traffic. This involved a roundabout journey and it is not surprising that the venture ultimately failed, after which no passenger vessels plied on the river for many years.

Under the two Balfour brothers, Arthur J. ('Bloody Balfour') and Gerald, who were successively Chief Secretary for Ireland between 1886 and 1891, and 1895 and 1900, the British government developed a policy of 'killing Home Rule by kindness'. As the nickname suggests, there was in fact a good deal of repression in that kindness, but nonetheless the government did spend what were by late Victorian standards quite large sums of public money in an attempt to improve the economy of the poorer areas. Much of this was administered through a new organisation called the Congested Districts Board, whose Chairman was the Chief Secretary himself. It had an initial budget of £41,000, a large sum for the time, and in due course it used some of this to set

Countess Cadogan was built for the Shannon Development Company by Bow, MacLachlan of Paisley in 1897 and remained on the Shannon until 1913. She then moved to Lough Corrib, but her service there was brief as all services on this lough were suspended at some point during the 1914-18 war and were not resumed thereafter. *Countess Cadogan* then returned to Scotland and was operated at Aberdeen until 1932. *Author's collection*

"S.S. Countess Cadogan" River Shannon.

up the Shannon Development Company, with a grant of £9,500; subsidies were also received from the M&GWR and other railways, as well as from the local authorities that covered the area.

The aim was to develop a year-round service of passenger steamers on the Shannon, with considerable provision of tourist services in summer. No fewer than six steamers were then acquired, three built new, and an ambitious timetable was put into operation on 18 June 1897. With this it was possible for tourists who did not mind spending two days on board the ships to cover the 108 miles from Carrick-on-Shannon to Killaloe. There was also a ferry service on Lough Derg. Prince George and Princes May obligingly took a trip from Killaloe to Banagher on *Countess of Mayo* in 1898 and thereafter the services were marketed under he slogan of 'The Duke of York Route'.

However, even this royal patronage did not guarantee success, and by 1909 four of the ships had been sold and the services operated had come down to a summer-only timetable for the 36 miles between Banagher and Killaloe. Circular tours were operated by the G&SWR from Dublin at a fare of 13 shillings, which covered rail travel to Banagher, the river trip with lunch on board, and return by rail from Killaloe. With a start at 9.15am and a return to Kingsbridge at 10.40pm, it could have been an exhausting day out! At all events, patronage of the steamers declined, and even before the First World War there were signs of competition from the roads. The last trips were run in 1913 and the remaining steamers sold.

Sailings then lapsed until June 1955, when CIE

decided to place one motor vessel on the river. This was *St Brendan*, which had originated in Paris in 1937 and had then been on the Thames. Appropriately enough for a ship named after an ocean-going saint, she crossed the Irish Sea under her own power. She proved successful and in 1956 was joined by *St Ciaran* from the Norfolk Broads. Regular services were offered from Killaloe, and now the ships were used to complement road services instead of competing with them. CIE had begun to develop its inclusive coach tours, using the splendid U Class Leyland Royal Tigers, which entered service from 1954 onward, and many of these incorporated a cruise on the Shannon as part of the itinerary. There were also day trips by road from Dublin to Athlone, from which a lunch cruise was offered to Clonmaenoise.

The lower Shannon would seem to offer opportunities for pleasure sailing, and various steamers plied on it until the First World War. These were mainly passenger ships and, as winter sailings were discontinued as early as the 1870s, it may be assumed that many of the passengers used the steamers for pleasure trips. The City of Dublin SP Company operated ships at an early date, and William Dargan, the builder of many Irish railways, began running an opposition fleet in 1850. The City Company then withdrew and in 1861 Dargan sold his ships to William Malcolmson of the Waterford SS Company (qv), who was also Chairman of the Waterford & Limerick Railway. This company maintained the services until 1907, when the remaining ships were transferred to the Limerick SS Company. The ships sailed from Limerick to Kilrush with intermediate calls, and at the latter pier connected with the trains of the narrow gauge West Clare Railway, which ran a special 'Steamer Express' from the pier to Kilkee. Through fares were available. Attempts to revive the Shannon steamers after 1918 proved fruitless and it was not until the recent arrival of car ferries that it was once again possible to enjoy a trip on the estuary.

Top **St Brendan** with a capacity crowd on the Shannon in the 1950s. *CIE and Heritage Officer, Iarnrod Eireann*

Middle **St Ciaran** near Athlone. *CIE and Heritage Officer, Iarnrod Eireann*

Left The U Class coaches, which connected with these sailings, were named after rivers, and **The Bride** is seen here amid the gorse. *CIE and Heritage Officer, Iarnrod Eireann*

One of the Waterford company's steamers was *Mermaid*, which had begun life in 1864 as *Largs*, part of the initial fleet of the Wemyss Bay Railway Company on the Clyde. She was sold to the Waterford company in 1875 and immediately placed on the Shannon, where she remained until withdrawn in 1903. This photograph was taken at Waterford. *Courtesy of National Library of Ireland*

Belfast Lough

Belfast was, in the late 19th century, the only city in Ireland that seemed to offer the right conditions to support a thriving service of pleasure steamers along the lines of those on the Clyde or the Isle of Wight area. It had a fairly large middle class and also an increasingly affluent working class, the River Lagan itself offered plenty of interest, and the services could be enjoyed without the need to make a long rail journey to reach the starting point.

The first ship to offer cruises on the Lough was also the first to operate between Scotland and Ireland. On 19 April 1816 the paddle steamer *Greenock* crossed from Campbeltown to Belfast in 11 hours and remained for about a month, during which she ran excursions to Bangor. Subsequently many other steamers operated on the lough, the principal operator from 1852 being J. & R. Brown/John Brown & Company, which in 1887 became the Belfast, Bangor & Larne Steamboat Company. In 1893 the Belfast & County Down Railway placed its first steamer on the Lough, and after one season of fruitless competition the older company sold out to the newcomer. The latter maintained the services until late 1915, and after 1918 sailings were given only on an irregular basis by private operators, mainly those of the ocean liner tenders stationed at Belfast.

One of the steamers taken over by the B&CDR, but not used by it, was *Bangor Castle*, built, as *Palmerston*, in Glasgow by T. & W. Wingate in 1864, which had arrived at Belfast from the Thames in 1873. Her name was changed to suit her new employment in 1877. Apart from her regular run to Bangor, she also gave occasional cruises to Larne and made cross-channel trips to Scotland. By 1893 she was distinctly old-fashioned and the B&CDR sold her to owners in Plymouth, where she lasted until 1899. In 1889 she was chartered by the Southampton & Isle of Wight Company (today's Red Funnel Line) to stand in following the loss of that company's new *Princess of Wales* during her trials on the Clyde. This view shows her leaving Portsmouth harbour during that year. *McLean Museum & Art Gallery, Inverclyde Council*

Above Not knowing much about the operation of pleasure steamers, the railway went for advice to the Glasgow & South Western Railway in Scotland, which was in the process of developing its Clyde fleet. The G&SWR had ordered one paddle steamer from J. & G. Thomson of Clydebank, and the builder, no doubt hoping to tempt the company with an offer of two ships for less than the cost of two individual vessels, laid down a second one. The G&SWR dithered a bit, and this second ship was snapped up by the B&CDR, which named her *Slieve Donard.* This is probably a trial view from the Clyde. *McLean Museum & Art Gallery, Inverclyde Council*

Below On 20 June 1893 *Slieve Donard* made her first sailing under the command of Captain Dalzell Torrance and the travelling public responded with enthusiasm to the new venture, which offered a far higher standard of comfort than the older ships had done. But some of the novelty seemed to wear off after a few years and the number of departures from Belfast came down from seven to four per day. *Slieve Donard* was then sold to P. & A. Campbell Ltd for Bristol Channel services. Re-named *Albion,* she lasted until 1921, but her excellent machinery soldiered on until 1957 in the new *Glen Gower.* In this view she is approaching the pier that served the Bangor Boat at Belfast. On the left is one of the Fleetwood steamers and ahead of her is *Magic. Author's collection*

Donegall Quay, Belfast.

BANGOR BOAT ARRIVING AT NEW PIER, BANGOR

Above With prospects apparently so rosy, the B&CDR lost no time in ordering a second ship from Thomson, and *Slieve Bearnagh* arrived in time for the 1894 season. Six departures could then be given per day, one of the afternoon sailings continuing to Larne. She was larger than *Slieve Donard* and her promenade deck extended to the bow. With two ships in service, excursions could be offered to Portrush, Donaghdee and even Strangford Lough. She carried on the service alone after 1899, giving three sailings per day. Return fares were 1s 6d or 1 shilling, and tickets could be used to return by rail. In 1911 she was offered for sale, at a rather optimistic £12,000. No interest was shown and she finally went off to D. & J. Nicholl of Dundee in June 1912 for £4,350. This postcard shows her coming alongside the pier at Bangor. *Author's collection*

Below The reason for selling off *Slieve Bearnagh* was that it had been decided to order a larger and finer ship, for which the order went to A. & J. Inglis of Glasgow, builders of many ships for the North British Clyde services. *Erin's Isle* arrived in Ireland just in time for the 12 July holidays of 1912, and for four years was most successful on the Bangor run. She made her last sailing in September 1915 and was then called up for war service, as a minesweeper. On this duty she was sunk, and as the Admiralty offered only £53,676, the railway, having found that a new ship would now cost £64,000, decided not to replace her. In this view she is passing one of the coal depots that were a feature of Belfast harbour for many years, and a typical collier can be seen behind her. *McLean Museum & Art Gallery, Inverclyde Council*

THE FERRY, BELFAST HARBOUR.

Above At one time the Belfast Harbour Commissioners operated ferries, of a design similar to that used in Glasgow. The three services were operated by the Harbour Commissioners and ran from Donegall Quay to Queen's Quay, Pilot Street and Alexandra Basin and at Milewater Basin. This view shows Ferry No 2 on the first of these services; this was the only one to survive into recent times and in 1970 was still running, worked by a privately owned motor launch. *Author's collection*

Below Bangor was also a destination for day excursions for the other side of the Irish Sea, and here the Heysham *Duke of Rothesay* of 1928 is seen leaving the pier. M. *Walker, Lancaster City Museums*

13752. BELFAST. DONEGALL QUAY — JUDGES LTD.

Above   Among the steamers that operated briefly on the Lough after 1918 was one that had already had a long connection with Ireland. The little paddle steamer *Cynthia* was built in 1892 for excursion work at Margate and, after passing through the hands of several owners in the South of England, she was sold in 1907 to the Moville Steamship Company for service between Derry and Moville, cruises to Portrush and Tory Island, and tender work at Moville. In 1928 she passed to the Anchor Line, but the number of liner calls at Moville was decreasing and in June 1931 she was sold again to Messrs Stewart & Hewitt of Belfast. She gave afternoon trips to Bangor and Donaghadee and occasional day trips to Larne. From Bangor she also offered 'tea dansant' cruises, on which passengers had tea, a non-landing cruise and a dance, all for 2s 6d. It would seem that her trips were not successful, since she was further sold in November 1931 to Dublin owners. After running from Dublin and Dun Laoghaire during 1932, she was laid up in the latter for the winter, and on 24 February 1933 was driven ashore and wrecked during a violent storm. Although passing through the hands of eight owners, her name was not changed at any time, nor was her appearance much altered, apart from the fitting of a saloon on her after deck while she was at Moville. She is seen here at the Belfast pier during 1931, when her funnel colouring was black with one blue band between two white bands. Also at Donegall Quay are steamers for Ardrossan, Glasgow, Heysham and Liverpool. *Author's collection*

Above   Although regular services along the coast of the north of Ireland have long ceased, it is still possible to enjoy the marvellous scenery on a few days each year, thanks to the operation of the preserved motorship *Balmoral*, which provides a range of excursions during her annual visit to the area. In this view, in June 2004, she is returning to the pier at Portaferry after a cruise on Strangford Lough, prior to returning to Peel in the Isle of Man. *Author*

18. SPECIAL OCCASIONS

As the prime means of transport between Britain and Ireland, when the two made one political unit, it was natural that the Irish Sea ships would be associated with the great and the good who made policy in the then United Kingdom, and that they would also have a role to play in the partial dissolution of that union and the events that followed.

The LNWR and Royalty

Although it did not carry any Royal passengers, the LNWR did have some close contacts with the royal family, mainly at Holyhead. When the new harbour was completed on 16 August 1873, the Prince of Wales agreed to perform the formal opening ceremony. He was accompanied by his brother, the Duke of Edinburgh, and travelled on the broad gauge quarry railway that had brought down stone to the harbour. He returned in June 1880 to open the station and hotel, and this visit was commemorated by the placing of a handsome clock in the area between the arrival and departure berths. Thoroughly renovated, this clock now stands outside Stena House.

Just 20 years later, in April 1900, his mother Queen Victoria passed through Holyhead en route to and from Ireland for her third (rather overdue) visit to Ireland, and although she travelled in her own yacht, *Victoria and Albert*, the occasion still brought considerable kudos to the railway and some captains entertained guests on board ship to mark the visit. All ships in harbour were dressed overall. The station was also converted to electric lighting at the time.

In 1887 the LNWR Board decided that Jubilee Day (21 June) should be a day's holiday with pay for all staff. *Banshee* was the ship chosen to represent the Premier Line and, while in the south, she was tried on the measured mile in Stokes Bay. She was at this time insured for

£40,000. All went off well and the crew were afterwards given two days extra pay as a reward for their good conduct.

When the naval review to mark Victoria's Diamond Jubilee was proposed, it was unfortunate that the new express steamer was not nearly ready and the LNWR could hardly be represented by the now out-of-date *Banshee*. Instead the Board decided to send the company's newest ship, *Connemara*, together with *Duke of Lancaster* and the little coastal paddle steamer *Lune* from Fleetwood. Mr MacCartney, an LNWR Director and Secretary to the Board of Admiralty, undertook to secure a good station for the ships, which at night were illuminated by rows of lights around their bulwarks and at mastheads, and the best Welsh smokeless coal was used. A through train was run from Euston to Southampton to convey guests of the company, and on Sunday 27 June the ships made a cruise around the Isle of Wight. All must have gone well, for some weeks later a special committee decided to award gratuities of £64 10s to the crews of the vessels concerned. For those who remained at their usual posts, there was the satisfaction of an extra day's pay.

A spectacular departure from Belfast

When she was very new, *Patriotic* was in the news on 28 September 1912 when she carried Sir Edward Carson and other prominent unionists from Belfast to Liverpool, at the start of their campaign against the Irish Home Rule Bill. Before she left Sir Edward made a speech from her promenade deck, ending with the words 'No surrender'. Her departure took place in a distinctly Wagnerian setting – as she proceeded down Belfast Lough she was illuminated by a searchlight mounted at Holywood on the eastern shore and

Patriotic as built. Author's collection

she passed many bonfire beacons lit by supporters of Sir Edward, who gave a spirited rendering of 'Oh God our help in ages past' at the appropriate moment. As she passed each of these, Captain Paisley sounded his ship's siren, and until she reached the open sea she was accompanied by the County Down's paddle steamer *Erin's Isle*. It was a choppy crossing but all reached Liverpool safely, where there were further speeches from waiting Unionists and further singing of 'Oh God our help'.

The ship was later involved with one consequence of Sir Edward's resistance. In due course the Government of Ireland Act (1920) was passed and as a result a parliament was set up in the north. This was opened by King George V on 22 June 1921, who made a conciliatory speech that paved the way for a truce in the south of the country. Unfortunately, when he came to leave the next morning, the tide was too low to allow the Royal Yacht to come alongside Donegall Quay, and she berthed down-river at Thompson's Wharf, to which land access was via the shipyard.

As the possibility of the King in the full uniform of an Admiral of the Fleet, and Queen Mary in a smart toque, tripping over a stray chain or rivet could not be contemplated, *Patriotic* was briefly chartered to act as a tender, the first and last occasion on which an Irish Sea ship has carried the reigning British monarch; for this duty her saloon was transformed into 'a veritable flower garden'. When the Royal trip was over, the steamer made a cruise down the Lough with a company of distinguished guests.

The creation of the Irish Free State

Apart from a brief period in the spring of 1916, when the City of Dublin Company's ships were requisitioned to carry troops from Liverpool to Dublin in the repression that followed the proclamation of the republic, Irish Sea ships were not actually much involved in the events unfolding in Ireland. Some prisoners taken during that period were transported to England in cargo

This early postcard bears a none-too-accurate depiction of one of the mail boats, labelled as *Munster*. The CDSPC houseflag, with Dublin's three castles, can clearly be seen. The message on the front of the card – writing on the back had not yet been permitted by the Post Office – says that 'Lady D and I arrived safely' and clearly shows the class of passenger that the mail boats often carried. 'Lady D' would no doubt have been surprised, had she crossed on 18 June 1917, to find that among her fellow passengers were Eamon de Valera and other prisoners just released by the British authorities. There was a great welcome for them at Kingstown, and as they came down the gangway they gave a rousing chorus of 'The Soldier's Song'. *Author's collection*

R.M.S. "MUNSTER"

Below Delegates setting out for London on 12 July 1921 to begin the negotiations for a truce that would ultimately lead to the creation of An Saorstat Eireann/the Irish Free State. In this picture, taken on board at Dun Laoghaire, are (left to right) Arthur Griffith, Robert Barton, Art O'Brien (possibly – his identity has not been definitely established), Count J.

M. Plunkett and Eamon de Valera. As negotiations for the treaty itself progressed, relations between delegates became somewhat strained and they often travelled on separate ships. On the day after the treaty was finally signed, the delegates returned by the 'Irish Mail' to Holyhead, where they boarded the new *Cambria*. Unfortunately the ship was not far out of Holyhead when, at 3.30am, she collided with a schooner from Arklow and put back to the port with the four survivors. Apparently General Collins took a lead in walking the decks and calming passengers who feared that *Cambria* herself had been damaged. The passengers finally reached Dun Laoghaire at 10.15am and the delegates had a rushed journey to the Mansion House in Dublin for a meeting of Dail Eireann at 11. They made it – just!
Courtesy of National Library of Ireland

Below The delegation is waved off by well-wishers and some curious bystanders at Dun Laoghaire. The cruiser stern of the ship makes it certain that she was *Curraghmore*.
Courtesy of National Library of Ireland

ships, but it is not now clear which ships were involved. However, a happier duty awaited one of the LNWR passenger ships when she carried delegates from Dail Eireann to discuss a truce in July 1921, following the King's appeal, as mentioned above.

De Valera's trips across the Irish Sea steadily improved in comfort as time went on. After the proclamation of the republic in 1916, he was transported to Britain in the hold of a cargo boat, in conditions somewhat reminiscent of the emigrant 'coffin' ships of the 1840s. As mentioned, he returned by mail boat, and when he was transported again to England in 1918 it was by warship. He returned from his second term in prison in February 1919, having escaped from Lincoln gaol and stowed away in the second mate's cabin on *Cambria*, this having been arranged by General Collins and supporters. When the accompanying photo was taken, he had graduated again to the (LNWR) mail boat, although it would appear that the group was travelling steerage, as they are standing at the stern of the ship. By the time he came over to Britain in 1938 to meet Neville Chamberlain, he had a special cabin at his disposal, and at Holyhead the ex-Midland Railway Royal Saloon awaited him.

The Civil War

Unfortunately the settlement reached in London in December 1921 was not accepted by all the people of Ireland, and in 1922 a Civil War began. The main thrust of the resistance was along a line running roughly from Limerick to Waterford, and the new government in Dublin decided to try to breach this line by landing troops at Cork. Not having any troopships of its own, it requisitioned the B&I *Lady Wicklow* and *Arvonia* from the LNWR. The latter sailed from North Wall on 7 August 1922, loaded with troops and some armoured cars, and duly reached Cork only to find that the opposition had blocked the channel by sinking Burns-Laird's *Gorilla* and a hopper. However, the captain managed to get round these and the troops were landed in Cork on 11 August.

Another to be caught up in this campaign was the steamer that was now *Killarney*, formerly the Belfast SS Company's *Magic*. As road and rail links out of Cork city were still both impassable, she had the melancholy honour of bringing back to Dublin the body of General Collins after his assassination on 22 August 1922.

Wicklow before her elevation to the nobility. *Glasgow University Archives*

Above Lady Wicklow as a troopship in 1922. *Courtesy of National Library of Ireland*

Below An armoured car being loaded aboard **Arvonia**. *Courtesy of National Library of Ireland*

A Royal occasion at Liverpool

The problem of reaching the Mersey from the dock was the main reason for the employment of three ships on the Liverpool to Belfast and Dublin services, and it had long been an aim of Coast Lines to be able to run these with only two ships each. This aim was finally realised in March 1950 when the new Waterloo entrance to Prince's Dock came into operation. It had been formally opened on 29 March 1949 by the present Queen, then Princess Elizabeth, accompanied by the Duke of Edinburgh. The couple sailed into the dock on board *Galatea*, the tender of the Mersey Docks &

Harbour Board, which cut a blue ribbon as she passed the entrance. *Ulster Prince*, with 300 guests of the Board, remained outside the dock and later met up with the Royal party at Salisbury Dock. In attendance also were the Wallasey ferry *J. Farley*, *Longford* and *Ulster Duke*. When the two-ship service was fully operational, the last of these became redundant, and on 8 March 1951 she was sold to Italian shipbreakers. However, she did not reach La Spezia, as she sank in the Bay of Biscay while under tow, taking with her three of the crew. It was a sad end to a long and distinguished career, and it may be that she resented being 'tugged to her last berth'.

Right *Galatea,* **with the Princess and the Duke on board, enters the new lock.** *H. B. Christiansen*

Below Out in the Mersey, *Longford,* dressed overall, waits to greet the distinguished visitors. *H. B. Christiansen*

19. ACCIDENTS WILL HAPPEN

Accidents will happen – but some ships seem to be more accident-prone than others!

One of those was certainly the Heysham steamer *Duke of Lancaster* of 1928. She had been in service for only six months when she was stranded at Heysham, and in May 1930 she collided with her sister *Duke of Rothesay* at Belfast. Then, as she was lying at No 2 berth at Heysham preparing to sail for Belfast on the evening of Friday 27 November 1931, a fire was discovered in a two-berth cabin on the starboard side of deck C, at the after end. Fire engines from Morecambe were soon on the scene, but by that time the whole of the after end of the ship was well alight and it was clear that she would not be sailing for Belfast that night! She was then moved back into No 3 berth and her sister *Duke of Argyll* moved to take her place. By the time additional fire appliances arrived from Lancaster and other places, the entire ship was blazing. There were no casualties, but unfortunately the Chief Fire Officer of Morecambe, Arnold Wilson, broke his arm while directing operations in the early hours of Saturday morning. So much water was pumped into the ship that she heeled over away from the quay and settled down on her starboard side, putting No 3 berth out of use for several weeks. At high tide only her masts and funnels were visible.

Princess Victoria came down from Stranraer to assist, but, with her limited sleeping accommodation, it could not have been an easy Christmas season for the Heysham staff. The Liverpool & Glasgow Salvage Association was called in to raise the ship and did so by using pontoons to which were attached heavy steel hawsers. These were then passed round the hull of the derelict, but some broke under the strain of lifting her. Finally, on the night of 15 January 1932, she came to an upright position and was beached at the east end of the harbour for a thorough inspection and to allow leaks to be closed. On 6 February *Wyvern* towed her back to Dumbarton, where she was totally rebuilt by

After the fire of November 1931, **Duke of Lancaster** lies on her side in Heysham harbour. *Lancaster City Museums*

Denny at a cost of £107,000, almost half her original cost. She re-entered service on 9 June.

The exact cause of the fire was not established, but it was thought to have originated with a cigarette end dropped by a workman. However, in 1972 the author E. H. Cookridge, in a book entitled *Spy of the Century*, alleged that the fire was part of a concerted campaign waged against British and French shipping by a communist spy, Ernst Wollweber, who had contacts with the IRA. Unlike other fires, such as that of the French liner *L'Atlantique*, no evidence of arson was found, and on the whole the idea seems unlikely: the saboteurs went for more important targets than a cross-channel ship.

It was not long before the *Duke* had some further adventures. In August 1932 she ran aground on Copeland Island in a fog, but was easily refloated, and in 1934 she had an argument with a trawler in Morecambe Bay. In June 1937 she ran hard on to the beach at Bride, near Point of Ayre in the Isle of Man. Passengers were landed in the lifeboats and the ship was refloated the next day. On 13 January 1940 she collided with and sank the coaster *Fire King* off the Isle of Man and had herself to be towed back to Heysham. One crew member of the coaster was lost.

Apart from some trooping in September 1939, her war service did not begin until January 1944 when she went up to the Clyde to be converted for use as a hospital ship. In this role she performed

Above Ashore at Bride, Isle of Man, in June 1937. M. Walker, Lancaster City Museum

Below The coaster *Fire King*. Courtesy of National Museums Liverpool, Merseyside Maritime Museum

very well and the only minor incident was the bursting of a boiler tube at Tilbury on Christmas Eve 1944. Apart from bringing back thousands of casualties to England, *Duke of Lancaster* rescued survivors from the hospital ship *Amsterdam* on 7 August 1944 and from four minesweepers on 27 August. She was one of the first cross-channel vessels to resume commercial service, on 12 December 1945, and thereafter led a blameless existence until withdrawn in October 1956.

Like ships, some places seem to have more accidents than others! The North Channel between Scotland and Ireland was one of these.

The handsome vessel *Rowan* was one of the last two to be built for the Laird Line, in 1909. Accommodation for passengers travelling cabin comprised a small lounge on the upper deck, a dining saloon forward on the promenade deck, a smoke room aft on the same deck, and cabins on that and the main deck. For those in steerage, there was a ladies' lounge in the poop deckhouse and a general room below. She was employed on the services from Glasgow to Derry and Dublin, and it was on the latter that she met her end, on the foggy night of 8 October 1921.

Rowan on the Clyde. *Courtesy of National Museums Liverpool, Merseyside Maritime Museum*

In the days before air travel, actors and musicians were an important group of year-round passengers on cross-channel ships. On the day in question, a jazz group known as the Southern Syncopated Orchestra was performing at a matinée in the Lyric Theatre in Glasgow and had arranged to proceed by train to Greenock to board *Rowan* for onward passage to Dublin. The audience was appreciative and demanded encores, and as a result the group was late in arriving at Greenock. However, Captain Brown waited for them and the ship finally set off more than an hour late, only to run into thick fog when she reached the North Channel. At about half her normal speed, *Rowan* continued on her journey and just after midnight was hit on the stern by the US Shipping Board's *West Camak*. As a precaution, passengers were mustered on deck, life jackets issued and the boats made ready, but unfortunately the ship's whistle was not sounded. It was as well that Captain Brown had been so careful, since within minutes *Rowan* was struck again, this time on the starboard side amidships by the cargo liner *Clan Campbell*. *Rowan* sank immediately, having been almost cut in two, and her passengers were thrown into the water, there being no time to launch the boats. However, the other two ships involved and a destroyer that was quickly on the

scene managed to rescue no fewer than 77 people, about 20 being lost. Sadly Captain Brown was one of these, as were some members of the band. It was a nasty accident but, had the passengers been left in their beds when the first collision took place, it would have been a great deal worse.

This was not the first accident to befall Clyde cross-channel ships in the North Channel, and it was not to be the last. On 22 December 1929 the Burns Laird ship *Lairdselm*, outward bound to Belfast with a cargo of diesel engine sections for Harland & Wolff, took shelter in Loch Ryan during the night, as the captain had found problems maintaining the trim of the ship. This problem had worsened by the morning, and at 9.30 the crew abandoned the vessel, which soon afterwards sank. No lives were lost and it is possible that some of the cargo was later salvaged, although the exact fate of the wreck remains a mystery.

Fog was to claim another three victims in this area just eight years later, although in only two cases were the consequences serious. The almost-

new cargo motorship *Lairdsbank* ran aground in thick fog on the Mull of Galloway on 6 April 1937 while en route from Derry to Heysham. She was badly holed and a first attempt at salvage failed. The Portpatrick lifeboat rescued seven cattle drovers, but the 200 cattle and 200 pigs remained aboard until the ship was refloated on the next high tide, reaching Ayr safely under her own power. The animals were all safe and sound and the ship herself was soon repaired at Troon.

Incredibly, the next accident came only one day later. On the morning of 7 April *Lairdsmoor* was inbound from Dublin with 33 crew, six passengers and 321 head of cattle. At 3.20am, a few miles west of Portpatrick, she was struck amidships by the Shaw Savill Line's motor vessel *Taranak*, sinking in half an hour. The passengers and all but two of the crew were rescued by the latter before the ship sank, the master and one fireman being lost with

Lairdsbank at Heysham. She is being assisted by the tug *Wyvern*, part of whose stern can also be seen. *Lancaster City Museums*

the ship. She had been built for Burns in 1919 by A. & J. Inglis, but for reasons unknown the line refused delivery and she went to the City of Cork Steam Packet Co as *Killarney*, coming back to Burns as *Moorfowl* when Coast Lines took over in 1921. In 1929 she became *Lairdsmoor* and had an observation lounge fitted below the bridge in 1932.

When war broke out in 1939, both the Burns Laird motorships of the Glasgow-Belfast service were requisitioned and, to keep the route open, the company used the ships formerly on it, *Lairdsburn* and *Lairdscastle*. On 4 September 1940 the latter was outward bound for Belfast and, as was normal in wartime, had extinguished her navigation lights on leaving the inner Firth of Clyde. Somewhere between Ailsa Craig and the Mull of Kintyre she was in collision with the *Vernon City*, owned by Messrs Reardon Smith. It was a calm night and all 72 passengers and 29 crew

were able to escape in the lifeboats, to be rescued soon afterwards by a destroyer, but the ship herself was a total loss.

And then there was the question of the 'Carlingford Lough triangle'. This was thought to be the haunting ground of the ghost ship *Lord Blayney*, a wooden paddle steamer lost with all on board on the coast of North Wales on 18 December 1833, after crossing from Newry. Her spirit returned to Carlingford and she made several appearances just before other ships were wrecked in the area.

The first LNWR ship to come to grief in or near the mouth of Carlingford Lough was the paddle steamer *Eleanor*, the first ship built new for the Greenore route in 1873. On the foggy morning of 27 January 1881 she went ashore at Leestone Point, near Kilkeel, having missed the entrance to the Lough. Admiral Dent went over with some of

Above A view of **Lairdsmoor**. *Courtesy of National Museums Liverpool, Merseyside Maritime Museum*

Left **Lairdscastle** between 1930 and 1936. *Courtesy of National Museums Liverpool, Merseyside Maritime Museum*

the workshop staff from Holyhead, and the Carlingford Lough Commissioners sent their tug *Lord Derby* to try to pull her off, but she was unable to do so and, when bad weather set in, the wrecked ship broke up. The reserve steamer *Telegraph*, a veteran of the Crimean War, was sent up from Dublin to take her place, but she went aground at Cooley Point the same evening. Although she was salvaged, she must have been beyond economical repair and was broken up shortly afterwards. No lives were lost in either incident, but Captain Lewis of *Eleanor* had his certificate suspended for three months and Admiral Dent pressed the Commissioners of Irish Lights to place a buoy outside the bar, to guide incoming ships. They duly obliged with an automatic whistling buoy, which depended on the movement of the sea to whistle and was clearly no use at all in a calm sea! Much later, in 1931, the LMS cargo steamer *Slieve More* was to go aground in much the same way, but with less unfortunate results.

On 2 March 1896 the almost new *Rosstrevor* of the LNWR took a sudden sheer against her helm when crossing the bar at the entrance to the Lough and grounded on it. All her passengers were taken off safely, although six horses and two cows were drowned, and the ship was beached to prevent her sinking. Captain Binney, now head of the LNWR's service, went over to assess the situation for himself and in due course wired Ismay, Imrie & Company to arrange for salvage. *Rosstrevor* was refloated on 7 March and taken to Holyhead, then Greenock and finally Dumbarton, where she was repaired by Denny on a basis of cost plus 15% on

materials and 10% on labour. Captain R. Thomas, aged 56 and only promoted from the cargo service in February 1895, was blamed for the accident and was relieved of his command. He was found alternative employment as night shore officer at Holyhead, at an annual salary of £150, just over half his previous earnings. This was perhaps a little unfair, as no satisfactory explanation was found for the behaviour of the ship. The LNWR Board was no doubt gratified that the Carlingford Lough Commissioners made no charge for the services of their tug and, in an outburst of generosity, gave them a donation of £10 5s 0d. They also paid 10 guineas to the RNLI and gave a week's pay to all hands of the *Rosstrevor* and to those of the local steamer *Severn*, which had assisted.

Much worse was to come in Carlingford Lough. On the stormy night of 3 November 1916 *Rosstrevor*'s sister *Connemara* left Greenore with 51 passengers, 17 of whom were young women going to Britain en route to Canada, where they hoped to find work as servants. There were also three drovers, a luggage guard and 31 crew. *Connemara* was under the command of Captain G. Doeg, her master since 1914. She left her berth punctually at 8.00pm, and at 8.28 passed Haulbowline lighthouse. Inbound at the same spot and battling against a strong ebb tide of 4.5 knots was the collier *Retriever*, of the Clanrye Shipping Company of Newry, which had crossed form Liverpool in stormy though not exceptional

Rosstrevor at sea. *McLean Museum & Art Gallery, Inverclyde Council*

The black Mournes sweeping down to the sea provide a pleasing backdrop for *Connemara* as she comes into Greenore. *McLean Museum & Art Gallery, Inverclyde Council*

conditions. In accordance with wartime practice, the navigation lights had not been lit when darkness fell, but the crew were about to do so as they entered inshore waters; conversely, *Connemara* was coming down the Lough with all lights lit, ready to be extinguished when she crossed the bar. Captain Patrick O'Neill of the collier was on the bridge, as he always personally commanded the ship at this point, and a young crew member, James Boyle, having attended to the port light, was making up the stove in his cabin. What happened next is not entirely clear, but it appears that *Retriever* suddenly sheered to port and struck the LNWR ship amidships at an angle of about 45 degrees, tearing a hole in her side that was in places 7 feet wide. Both ships sank in about 10 minutes, and the sole human survivor was James Boyle, who managed to reach the north shore and was picked up by some local residents who had heard explosions and had come down to investigate. It is likely that some cattle also made it to safety. Ninety-four people died.

It seemed incredible that a disaster of this magnitude could happen so close to land – James Boyle was actually wading ashore when rescued – and the reason for the loss of life probably rests with the almost total lack of preparedness on the part of those who were supposed to cope with such an emergency. The head keeper of Haulbowline light was ashore and the two men on duty, who witnessed the collision, fired detonators but not the emergency rockets. A member of the Greenore

lifeboat crew heard one of the detonations, but, not hearing any more, did not turn out, and a second member, who did hear them, seems not to have known what they meant. The coastguard on duty in the area was at a wake, the Royal Irish Constabulary was not informed, and the people from Cranfield, who had rescued Boyle, did not try to contact the authorities. The Carlingford Lough Commissioners almost new tug, *Slieve Fox*, had been requisitioned by the Admiralty. It was not until the Saturday morning, when *Galtee Mor* arrived from Holyhead, that it became clear that both ships had been lost.

It was a sorry tale of muddle and the subsequent court of enquiry considered that more lives could have been saved had some sort of organised rescue effort been made in the vicinity of Cranfield Point. From London, King George V and his consort sent a telegram of condolence to the LNWR Chairman, but made no gesture to the relatives of those who had perished. For them a disaster fund was set up, administered by the National Disasters Relief Council. There were many calls on it.

At a time when the Battle of the Somme was winding down to its dismal conclusion, the disaster attracted little notice nationally. No doubt many of the sons of Ulster, who fought with such gallantry in it, had used the Greenore route on their way to the front.

Relatives of Boyle reported having seen *Lord Blayney* on the day before the disaster...

20. MANXMAN,
THE LAST OF THE LINE

Isle of Man steamers are, of course, Irish Sea ships, and serve Ireland, thus they deserve a mention in a book of this kind. What more fitting conclusion could there be than to have a look at *Manxman*, the last classic steamer to operate on any cross-channel service around the coasts of Britain and Ireland and one for which there is still a hope of preservation. The accompanying photographs were all taken by the author to show something of the on-board atmosphere of a traditional cross-channel day steamer and as a tribute to a great ship and her crew. It is hoped that they will also salute those who are doing so much to preserve her as she deserves. At the time of writing, her future is by no means assured.

In March 1968, at a time when she still helped out with winter schedules, *Manxman* lies alongside the Pier Head in Liverpool.

Above left A view of the upper deck, with the siren in action, on passage from Douglas to Liverpool in July 1971.

Above The following six photographs were taken during a day trip from Fleetwood to Douglas in August 1982. One pleasing feature of the Isle of Man steamers was that passengers were permitted to go right up to the bow, an area normally out of bounds on cross-channel ships. Health and safety officers would not have approved – but on a fine day it was a delightful spot.

Left The wheelhouse, complete with traditional wheel and other fittings.

Opposite above left The magnificent triple-chime siren tells all of Fleetwood that she is about to leave port.

Opposite above right Looking aft over the stern. The three legs of Man can just be made out on the red ensign.

Right A view of the promenade deck. At TT Race times, this space would be crammed with motor cycles, while at other times cars were accommodated here.

Above In the Mersey, en route to Douglas.

Below The ship at Preston in July 1988, the first part of her journey downhill. The garish livery speaks for itself, but she still manages to maintain something of her old dignity.

Tailpiece

An evening shot on the Irish Sea: *Lady of Mann* trails her log en route from Douglas to Liverpool on 15 July 1970. *Author*

BIBLIOGRAPHY

General

Bourke, Edward J. *Shipwrecks of the Irish Coast* (Dublin, published by the author, 1994)

Campbell, C. and Fenton, R. *Burns and Laird* (Preston, Ships in Focus Publications, 1999)

Duckworth, C. L. D. and Langmuir, G. E. *Clyde and other Coastal Steamers* (2nd ed; Prescot, T. Stephenson & Sons, 1977)
Railway and other Steamers (Glasgow, Shipping Histories Ltd, 1948)

Forsythe, R. N. *Irish Sea Shipping Publicised* (Stroud, Tempus Publishing Ltd, 2002)

Freight Services to and from Northern Ireland (Belfast, Ministry of Commerce, 1962)

Haresnape, Brian *Sealink* (London, Ian Allan Ltd, 1982)

Irish Passenger Steamship Services, Vols 1 & 2 (Newton Abbot, David & Charles, 1969 and 1971)

Kennedy, Mark *The LMS in Ireland* (Leicester, Midland Publishing, 2000)

Liddle, Laurence *Passenger Ships of the Irish Sea, 1919-1969* (Newtonards, Co Down, Colourpoint Books, 1998)

Lyon, David J. *The Denny List* (London, National Maritime Museum, 1975)

McRonald, Malcolm *The Irish Boats, Volume 1: Liverpool to Dublin* (Stroud, Tempus Publishing Ltd, 2005)

Ripley, Don and Regan, Tony *Designing Ships for Sealink* (Ramsey, Ferry Publications, 1995)

Sinclair, Robert C. *Across the Irish Sea: Belfast-Liverpool Shipping since 1819* (London, Conway Maritime Press, 1990)

Vale, E. *Ships of the Narrow Seas* (London, London, Midland & Scottish Railway, c1937)

Winser, John de S. *Short Sea, Long War: Cross-Channel Ships in World War II* (Gravesend, World Ship Society, 1997)

Chapter 1

Cameron, Stephen *Death in the North Channel* (Newtonards, Co Down, Colourpoint Books, 2002)

MacHaffie, Fraser G. *The Short Sea Route* (Prescot, T. Stephenson & Sons Ltd, 1975)

Chapter 2

Cowsill, Miles *Stranraer-Larne: The Car Ferry Era* (Ramsey, Ferry Publications, 1996)
   By Road across the Sea. The History of the Atlantic Steam Navigation Company (Ramsey, Ferry Publications, 1990)

Cowsill, Miles and Hendy, John *Holyhead-Dun Laoghaire: From Car Ferry to HSS 1965-1996* (Ramsey, Ferry Publications, 1996)

Merrigan, Justin *Car Ferries of the Irish Sea, 1954-2004* (Newtonards, Co Down, Colourpoint Books, 2004)

Chapter 12

Back Track, Vol 20, No 7, July 2006 (Railway hotels)

Barrie, D. S. M. *The Dundalk, Newry & Greenore Railway* (Tandridge, Surrey, Oakwood Press, 1957)

Denny Contract Books (*Cambria*)

Hitches, Mike *The Irish Mail* (Stroud, Sutton Publishing Ltd, 2000)

'The Holyhead Route to Ireland' (*Sea Breezes*, January 1967)

Ireland, J. de C. *History of Dun Laoghaire Harbour* (Blackrock, Co Dublin, Edmund Burke, 2001)

The Irish Mail: Centenary 1848-1948 (London, The Railway Executive, 1948)

'The Irish Mail Ships' (*Ships Illustrated*, August 1967)

McCarthy, Vera *The Hero of Lisfinny* (Jasper Pyne) (Leaving certificate dissertation, 1991)

Minutes of LNWR committees dealing with shipping services, 1883-1898

Pearsall, A. W. H. and Davies, H. H. *The Holyhead Steamers of the LNWR* (London & North Western Railway Society, n/d)

The Railway Magazine, August 1906

Rowlands, G. *No Problem's Too Small - The story of the Marine Yard at Holyhead* (Holyhead, published by the author, 2003)

Every Picture Tells a Story (Holyhead, published by the author, 2005)

Rowlands, G. and Pritchard, A. *Trains and Boats and Planes – Holyhead Past and Present* (Holyhead, G. Rowlands, 2004)

Scott, Brian *Sealink and its Predecessors in Dublin* (Dublin, published by the author, 1989)

Ships of the Narrow Seas, a film made by the LMS including a journey on the 'Irish Mail' circa 1930 and a sea crossing from Holyhead to Dun Laoghaire (Video, Transport in Vision, 1991)

Stokes, Roy *Death in the Irish Sea: The sinking of the RMS Leinster* (Wilton, Co Cork, The Collins Press, 1998)

'70 Years of the Irish Mail' (*Sea Breezes*, January 1978)

Chapter 14

Clague, D. *Heysham Port – A Century of Manx and Irish Services* (Ramsey, Ferry Publications Ltd, 2004)

Cowsill, Miles *Fishguard-Rosslare* (Ramsey, Ferry Publications Ltd, c1990)

Delaney-Nash, Capt J. FNI *A Varied Childhood and Fifty Years at Sea* (Knebworth, Able Publishing, n/d)

Merrigan, J. and Cleare, B. *Let Go Fore and Aft* (Nautical Signals, 1996)

The Railway Magazine, September 1906

Chapter 15

MacElwee, Richard *The Last Voyages of the Waterford Steamers* (The Book Centre (Waterford) Ltd, 1992)

Chapter 16

Norman, K. J. *The Furness Railway* (Great Addington, Silver Link Publishing Ltd, 1994)

Chapter 17

Grimshaw, G. *British Pleasure Steamers 1920-1939* (London, Richard Tilling, 1945)

McNeill, D. B. *Coastal Passenger Steamers and Inland Navigations in the North of Ireland* (Transport Handbook No 3) (Belfast Transport Museum, 1961)
   Coastal Passenger Steamers and Inland Navigations in the South of Ireland (Transport Handbook No 6) (Belfast Transport Museum, 1965)

Chapter 18

Jones, N., Robinson, T. and Carr, C. *Holyhead's Royal Visit* (Bredbury, Foxline (Publications) Ltd, 2000)

Chapter 19

Moir, P. and Crawford, I *Clyde Shipwrecks* (Wemyss Bay, published by the authors, 1988)

INDEX